Ann Benson's BEADWEAR

Ann Benson's
BEADWEAR

Making Beaded Accessories
& Adornments

A STERLING/CHAPELLE BOOK
Sterling Publishing Co. Inc. New York

For Chapelle, Ltd.
Owner
Jo Packham

Staff
Trice Boerens
Jennifer Burnett
Gaylene Byers
Rebecca Christensen
Holly Fuller
Cherie Hanson
Holly Hollingsworth
Susan Jorgensen
Lorin May
Corinna Souder
Florence Stacey
Nancy Whitley
Cheryl Yearsley
Lorrie Young

Photographers
Kevin Dilley, Gary Rohman, and Ryne Hazen

The photographs in this book were taken at
Anita Louise's Bear Lace Cottage, Park City, Utah

The Cowboy Tradin' Post, Ogden, Utah

Edie Stockstill's home,
Salt Lake City, Utah

Their cooperation and trust is deeply appreciated.

For information on where to purchase specialty items in this book, please write to Customer Service Department, Chapelle Designers, 204 25th Street Suite 300, Ogden, UT 84401.

Library of Congress Cataloging-in-Publication Data Available

10 9 8 7 6 5 4 3 2 1

A Sterling/Chapelle Book

Published by Sterling Publishing Company, Inc.
387 Park Avenue South, New York, N.Y. 10016
© 1994 by Chapelle Ltd.
Distributed in Canada by Sterling Publishing
c/o Canadian Manda Group, P.O. Box 920, Station U
Toronto, Ontario, Canada M8Z 5P9
Distributed in Great Britain and Europe by Cassell PLC
Villiers House, 41/47 Strand, London WC2N 5JE, England
Distributed in Australia by Capricorn Link (Australia) Pty Ltd.
P.O. Box 6651, Baulkham Hills, Business Centre, NSW 2153, Australia
Manufactured in Hong Kong
All rights reserved

Sterling ISBN 0-8069-0793-2

Introduction

My Fellow Beadiacs,

Life is good; I have been blessed with another opportunity to indulge my bead fantasies. At the same time, I have the great privilege of acting as your tour guide through what I hope will be some very satisfying bead journeys.

Although it is my profession to do so, indulging in the creative process continues to be a mental oasis for me. It's like a vitamin; I need it every day, and I don't feel quite right without it.

So I thank you for allowing me to do this design work, and I fervently hope that it can bring you even a small portion of the pleasure that it brought me.

Bead on!

—Ann Benson

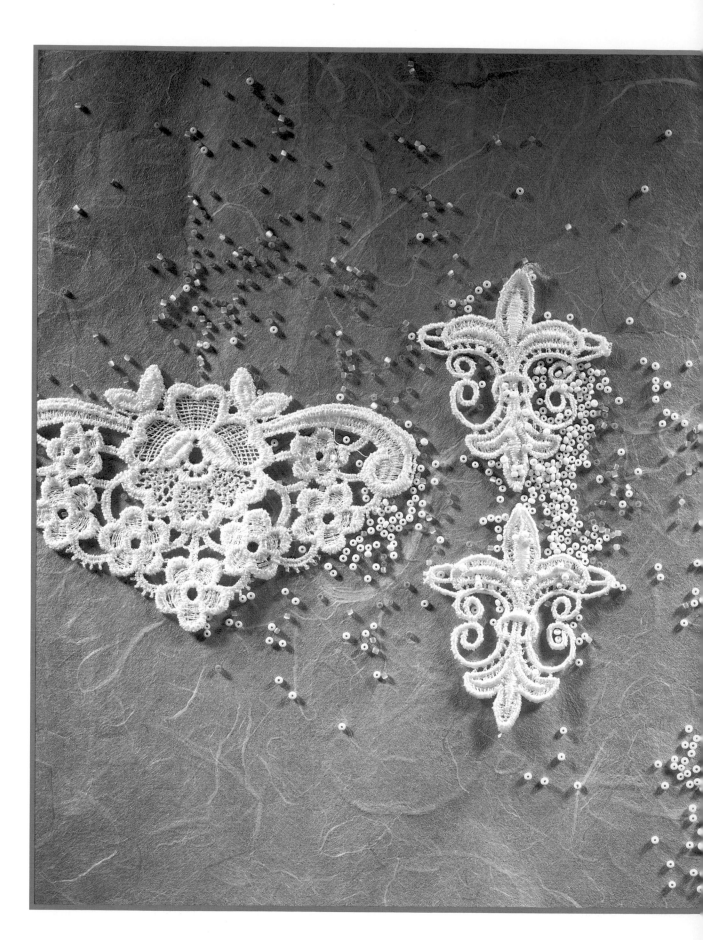

Contents

Chapter One

Denim Jacket

MATERIALS

One purchased denim jacket with chevron-shaped back yoke
Four silver 1¼" conchos with top hole
3 oz. metallic gold 11/0 seed beads
3 oz. metallic copper 11/0 seed beads
6 oz. opaque aqua 8/0 seed beads
3 oz. opaque lavender 8/0 seed beads
100 coral matte 6/0 seed beads
100 metallic copper 6/0 seed beads
3 oz. silver-lined gold #2 bugle beads

100 iris turquoise matte #2 bugle beads
40 frosted amethyst 10-mm donut-shaped disks with center holes
Nine 18-mm turquoise discs with center holes
22 lavender 6-mm ceramic cylinders
14 turquoise 8-mm discs with center holes
Scraps of leather: aqua, red, dark gold, gold, brown, and lavender
¼ yard of fusible webbing

DIRECTIONS

1. Make patterns. Adhere fusible webbing to back of leather scraps. Trace leather pattern onto back. Cut. Refer to General Instructions for "Fusing" on page 126.

2. Position shapes on jacket back; see diagram. Cover with clean white paper, pressing down for five seconds. Repeat until all are pressed. Press again for three seconds. Cool. Gently remove paper.

3. Outline sides of all lavender tail and wing feathers with aqua 8/0 seed beads. Backtrack.

4. Outline sides of all aqua tail and wing feathers with lavender 8/0 seed beads. Backtrack.

5. Outline outer edge of sections H and K with metallic gold 11/0 seed beads. Backtrack.

6. Outline bottom edges of sections B, D, E, F, and G with metallic gold 11/0 seed beads. Backtrack.

7. Outline sides of sections C, E, and G and outer edges of sections J and L with metallic copper 11/0 seed beads. Outline head and beak with metallic copper 11/0 seed beads. Backtrack.

8. Sew on all beads according to diagram.

9. Sew row of amethyst matte discs in the remaining spaces between sections D and E, and just inside wing feathers.

10. Sew conchos and bird's eye; see diagram.

11. Sew row of smaller turquoise discs anchored with metallic copper 11/0 seed beads in space above tail feathers.

12. Sew key pattern above yoke seam as shown in diagram. Space five patterns evenly between bird's head and shoulder seam.

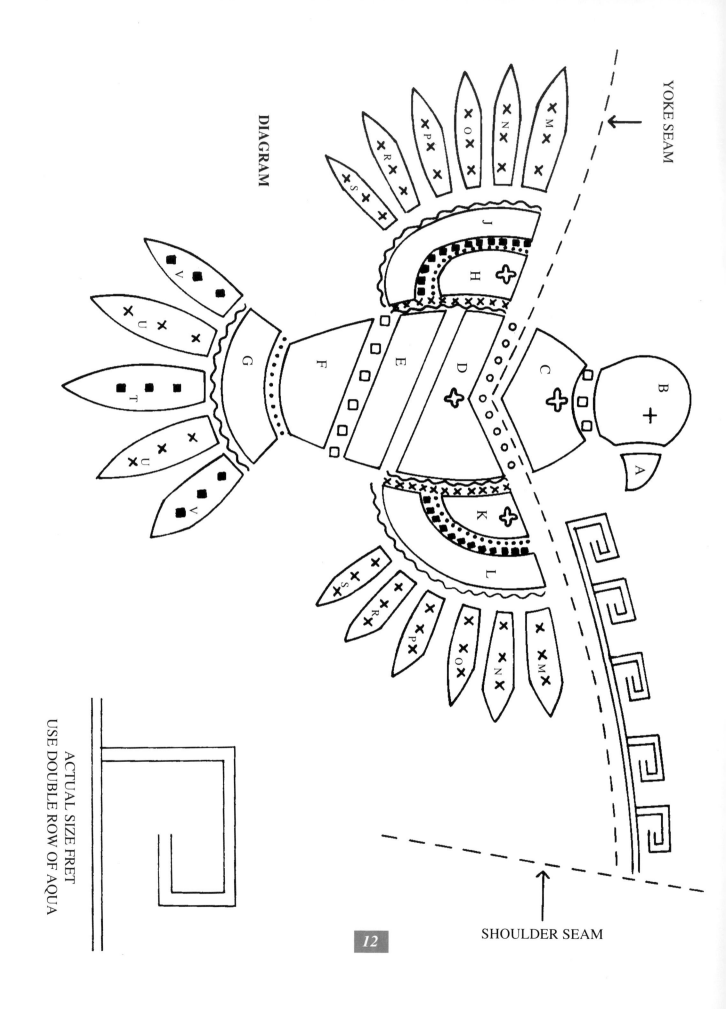

YOKE SEAM

DIAGRAM

SHOULDER SEAM

ACTUAL SIZE FRET
USE DOUBLE ROW OF AQUA

12

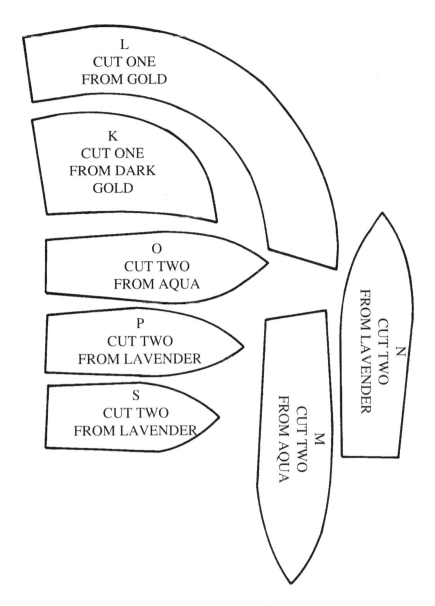

L
CUT ONE
FROM GOLD

K
CUT ONE
FROM DARK
GOLD

O
CUT TWO
FROM AQUA

P
CUT TWO
FROM LAVENDER

S
CUT TWO
FROM LAVENDER

N
CUT TWO
FROM LAVENDER

M
CUT TWO
FROM AQUA

■   METALLIC COPPER 6/0 SEED BEAD ANCHORED WITH METALLIC COPPER 11/0 SEED BEAD

x   CORAL MATTE 6/0 SEED BEAD ANCHORED WITH METALLIC COPPER 11/0 SEED BEAD

☐   18-MM TURQUOISE DISK ANCHORED WITH METALLIC COPPER 11/0 SEED BEAD

〰   ROW OF SILVER-LINED GOLD #2 BUGLE BEADS

⋯   ROW OF IRIS TURQUOISE MATTE #2 BUGLE BEADS

+   AMETHYST MATTE DISK ANCHORED WITH OPAQUE LAVENDER 8/0 SEED BEAD

⬦   SEW CONCHOS HERE

o   LAVENDER CERAMIC CYLINDER ANCHORED WITH GOLD 11/0 SEED BEAD

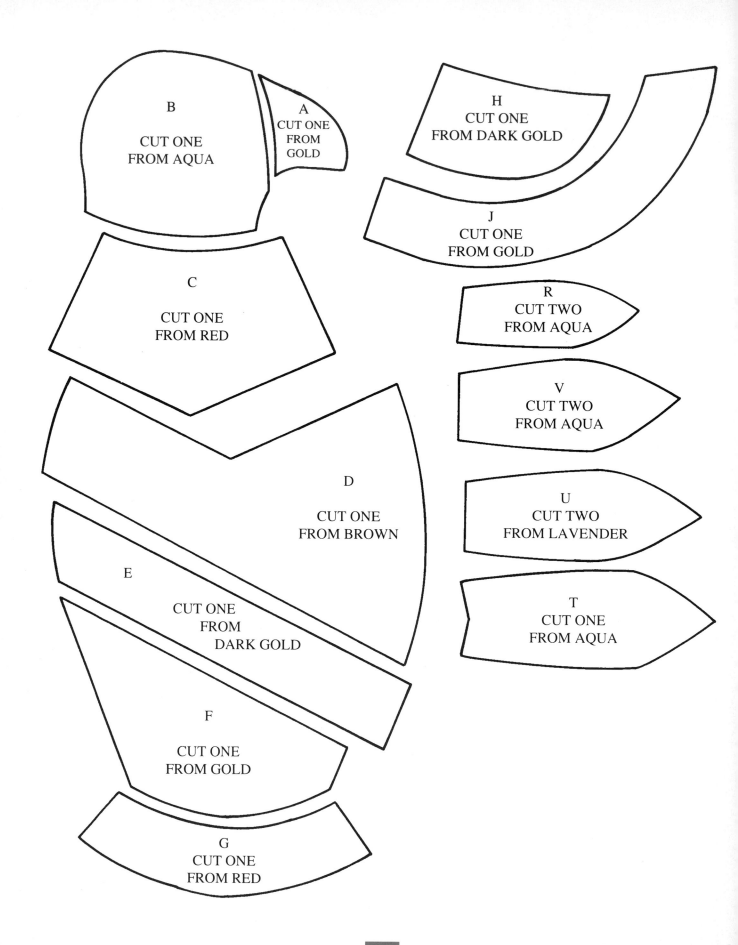

B

CUT ONE
FROM AQUA

A
CUT ONE
FROM
GOLD

H
CUT ONE
FROM DARK GOLD

J
CUT ONE
FROM GOLD

C

CUT ONE
FROM RED

R
CUT TWO
FROM AQUA

V
CUT TWO
FROM AQUA

D

CUT ONE
FROM BROWN

U
CUT TWO
FROM LAVENDER

E

CUT ONE
FROM
DARK GOLD

T
CUT ONE
FROM AQUA

F

CUT ONE
FROM GOLD

G
CUT ONE
FROM RED

Southwest Sweater

MATERIALS

One purchased crew- or turtleneck cotton knit sweater
Scraps of leather or ultrasuede: dark purple,
    lavender, moss green, brick, dusty blue, and bronze
600 opaque aqua 8/0 seed beads
550 opaque amethyst 8/0 seed beads
400 copper 6/0 seed beads

14 turquoise 8-mm flat discs
20 lavender flat ceramic discs
Three large, flat, odd-shaped turquoise chunks
Scraps of fusible webbing
Tracing paper

DIRECTIONS

1. Make leather patterns on pages 17 and 18. Adhere fusible webbing to back of leather scraps. Trace leather pattern onto back; cut. Refer to General Instructions for "Fusing" on page 126.

2. With sweater on flat surface, position leather; see diagram. Cover with clean white paper, pressing down for five seconds. Cool. Gently remove paper. Expect bronze leather to dull slightly after fusing.

3. Stitch beads to sweater, referring to beading guides and General Instructions for "Beading on Surfaces" on page 125.

NOTE: If sweater manufacturer recommends hand-washing, be sure to wipe excess water off leather surface immediately. The leather will not shrink, but may "wrinkle" slightly. When pressing, do not unfuse leather. Secure corners while beading.

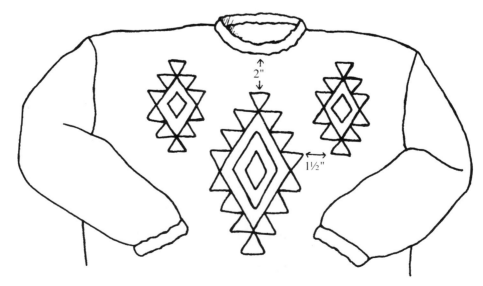

2"

1½"

DIAGRAM

CENTER PATTERN

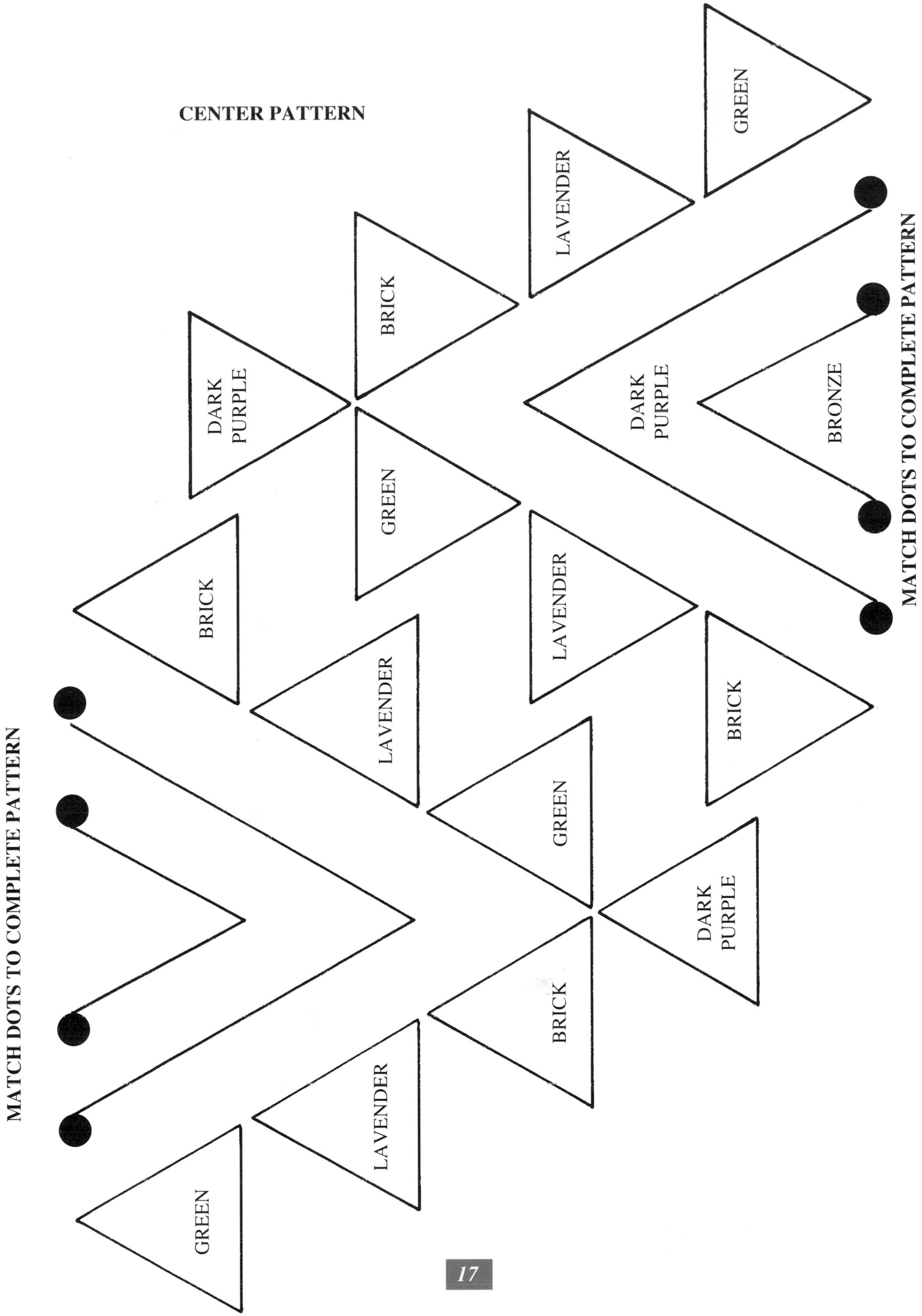

MATCH DOTS TO COMPLETE PATTERN

MATCH DOTS TO COMPLETE PATTERN

GREEN

LAVENDER

BRICK

DARK PURPLE

DARK PURPLE

BRONZE

GREEN

BRICK

LAVENDER

LAVENDER

BRICK

GREEN

DARK PURPLE

GREEN

BRICK

LAVENDER

17

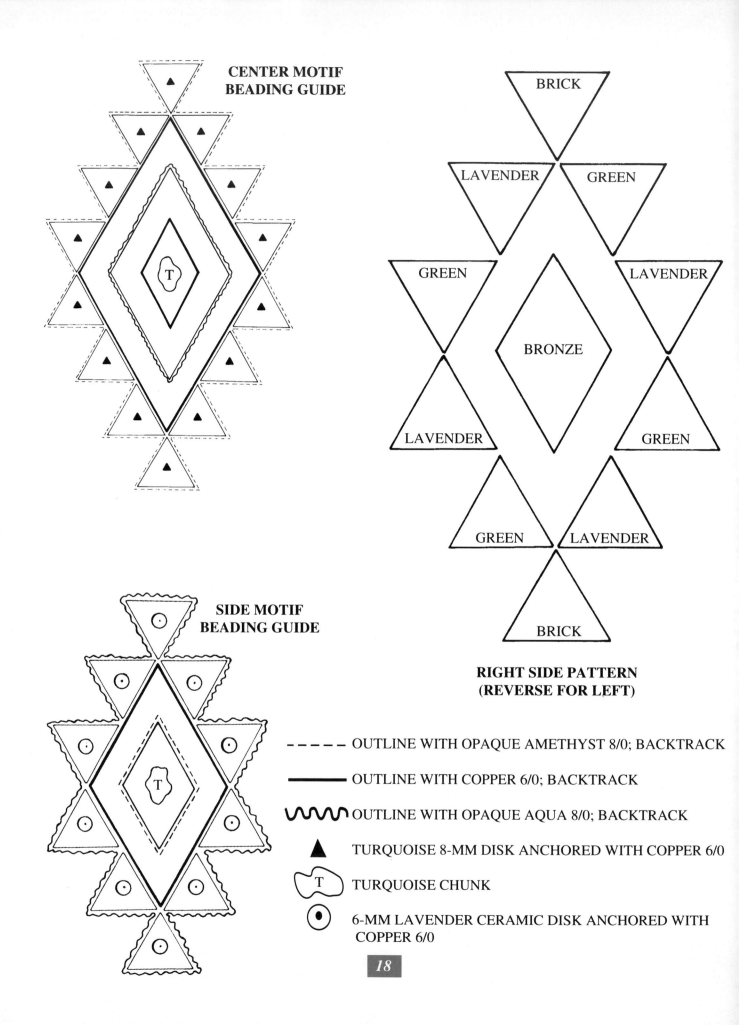

CENTER MOTIF BEADING GUIDE

T

BRICK

LAVENDER   GREEN

GREEN   LAVENDER

BRONZE

LAVENDER   GREEN

GREEN   LAVENDER

BRICK

RIGHT SIDE PATTERN (REVERSE FOR LEFT)

SIDE MOTIF BEADING GUIDE

T

– – – – – OUTLINE WITH OPAQUE AMETHYST 8/0; BACKTRACK

———— OUTLINE WITH COPPER 6/0; BACKTRACK

〜〜〜 OUTLINE WITH OPAQUE AQUA 8/0; BACKTRACK

▲ TURQUOISE 8-MM DISK ANCHORED WITH COPPER 6/0

T TURQUOISE CHUNK

⊙ 6-MM LAVENDER CERAMIC DISK ANCHORED WITH COPPER 6/0

_S_outhwest Denim Shirt

MATERIALS

One purchased shirt with pointed collar and two
    pockets with flaps
10/0 seed beads:
    1 oz. black
    1 oz. cream
    1 oz. red
    1 oz. green
    1 oz. light blue
    1 oz. aqua
    1 oz. pink

Two turquoise 10-mm chips
Turquoise discs or silver buttons (quantity and size to
    replace those on shirt)

DIRECTIONS

1. Remove existing buttons. Pre-shrink, following
manufacturer's instructions.

2. Transfer all patterns on page 21 to shirt.

3. Stitch beads onto shirt; see pattern. Replace buttons
with turquoise discs or silver buttons.

COLLAR POINT

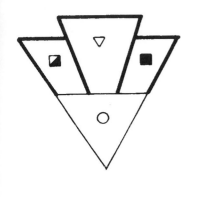

POCKET FLAP

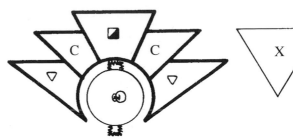

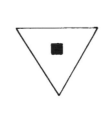

PLACKET
BUTTONHOLES

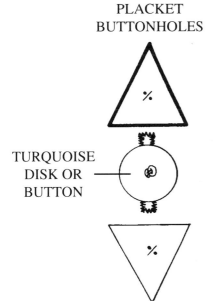

TURQUOISE
DISK OR
BUTTON

POCKET

SOUTHWEST DENIM SHIRT PATTERN

——	LINES OF CREAM 10/0 SEED BEADS	+++	LINES OF PINK 10/0 SEED BEADS
▬	LINES OF BLACK 10/0 SEED BEADS	■	FILL WITH AQUA 10/0 SEED BEADS
T	TURQUOISE 10-MM CHIP	▽	FILL WITH PINK 10/0 SEED BEADS
C	FILL WITH CREAM 10/0 SEED BEADS	◧	FILL WITH RED 10/0 SEED BEADS
X	FILL WITH GREEN 10/0 SEED BEADS	%	FILL WITH DESIRED COLOR
○	FILL WITH LIGHT BLUE SEED BEADS	▲	LINES OF RED 10/0 SEED BEADS

Bronze Earrings

3 oz. of metallic gold 12/0 three-cut beads
80 iris purple 12/0 three-cut beads
50 iris bronze 8/0 seed beads
76 iris matte light topaz #2 bugle beads
Eight AB finished topaz 4-mm glass beads
Two 8-mm carnelian beads

Four amethyst chips
Scrap of fabric
Scrap of fusible webbing
Bead card
Earring posts
Glue

DIRECTIONS

1. Transfer Bronze Earring Pattern on page 24 to bead card. Stitch beads according to pattern. (For your convenience, an enlarged pattern is provided below.)

2. Make fringe; see diagram. Work right to left for one earring; left to right for the other. Refer to General Instructions for "Fringes" on page 139.

3. Using beaded design piece as pattern, cut backing for each earring from fabric. Apply fusible webbing to wrong side of fabric. Fuse to wrong side of beadwork; refer to General Instructions for "Fusing" on page 126. Trim.

4. Glue earring posts to fabric.

ENLARGED PATTERN

BRONZE EARRING PATTERN

○   INDIVIDUAL METALLIC GOLD 12/0 THREE-CUT BEAD

────   IRIS MATTE LIGHT TOPAZ #2 BUGLE BEAD

········   LINES OF METALLIC GOLD 12/0 THREE-CUT BEADS

─ ─ ─   LINES OF IRIS BRONZE 8/0 SEED BEADS

Ⓐ   AMETHYST CHIP ANCHORED WITH METALLIC GOLD 12/0 THREE-CUT BEAD

• • • •   FRINGE PLACEMENT

DIAGRAM

□   METALLIC GOLD 12/0 THREE-CUT BEAD

⊡   IRIS PURPLE 12/0 THREE-CUT BEAD

▯   IRIS MATTE LIGHT TOPAZ #2 BUGLE BEAD

○   IRIS BRONZE 8/0 SEED BEAD

Ⓣ   AB FINISHED TOPAZ 4-MM GLASS BEAD

Ⓒ   8-MM CARNELIAN BEAD

Ⓐ   AMETHYST CHIP

24

Bronze Purse

MATERIALS

10" x 16" piece of 14-count interlock needlepoint canvas
¼" yard of lining fabric
200 yards of rayon or pearl cotton thread
One #20 tapestry needle

168 AB finished topaz #2 bugle beads
168 metallic silver 11/0 seed beads
3 oz. of metallic bronze 11/0 seed beads
Seven bronze 8-mm crystals
Two gold end caps

DIRECTIONS

All seams are ¼".

1. Stitch needlepoint pattern on page 27 onto canvas; see General Instructions for "Sewing on Needlepoint Canvas" on page 130. Trim.

2. Stitch beads onto finished needlepoint canvas; see pattern.

3. Make one pattern from finished needlepoint canvas. Cut one pattern from lining, adding ¼" to all edges. With wrong sides facing and turning all edges under ¼", hand-stitch lining to canvas. With right sides facing, fold short, straight edge up 5½". Hand-stitch side edges together, leaving top open.

4. Stitch one row of bronze 11/0 seed beads along seam line around entire purse. Using 21 bronze 11/0 seed beads, make a loop. Stitch loop to "V" on flap. Stitch 8-mm crystal bead in place; see diagram.

5. To make handle, cut four 20" lengths of thread. Thread bronze 11/0 seed beads on each strand. Handling all four strands as one, twist. Thread one end through end cap. Stitch to corner of back flap. Repeat with remaining end and end cap.

DIAGRAM

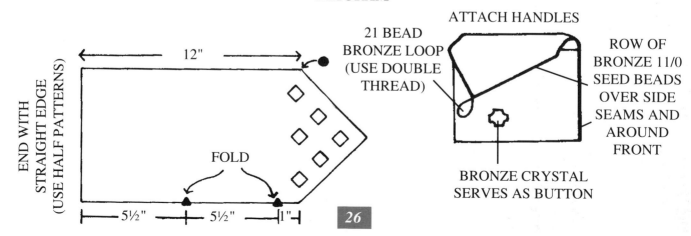

BASIC REPEAT

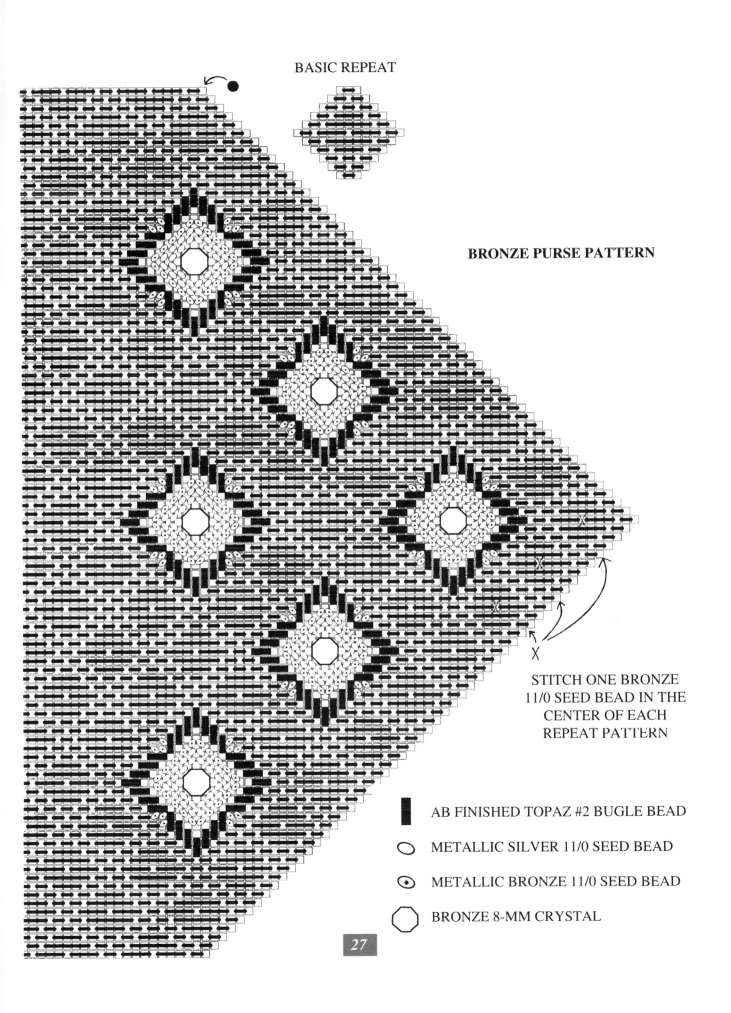

BRONZE PURSE PATTERN

STITCH ONE BRONZE
11/0 SEED BEAD IN THE
CENTER OF EACH
REPEAT PATTERN

▮ AB FINISHED TOPAZ #2 BUGLE BEAD

◯ METALLIC SILVER 11/0 SEED BEAD

◉ METALLIC BRONZE 11/0 SEED BEAD

⬡ BRONZE 8-MM CRYSTAL

ronze Epaulets

MATERIALS

11/0 seed beads
  2 oz. of bronze
  2 oz. of silver
  2 oz. of copper
  6 oz. of iris smoke matte
40 bronze 8-mm crystals

64 iris purple 5-mm x 7-mm crystal teardrops
162 iris bronze 6/0 seed beads
100 bronze #2 bugle beads
8" x 10" piece of gray felt
Tracing paper

DIRECTIONS

1. From felt, make two epaulet patterns on page 29, transferring all lines.

2. Stitch beads as indicated on pattern, filling in background.

3. To finish, trim excess felt. Wear epaulets across shoulders.

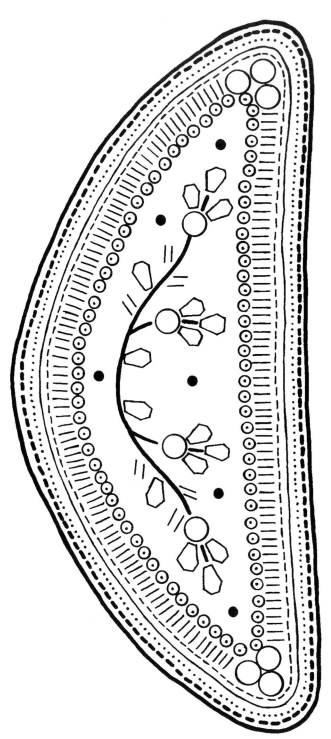

○ BRONZE 8-MM CRYSTAL

▬ LINE OF COPPER 11/0 SEED BEADS

▬ ▬ LINE OF ALTERNATING BRONZE AND COPPER 11/0 SEED BEADS

•••• LINE OF BRONZE 11/0 SEED BEADS

⬠ IRIS PURPLE 5-MM X 7-MM CRYSTAL TEARDROP

⊙ IRIS BRONZE 6/0 SEED BEAD ANCHORED WITH BRONZE 11/0 SEED BEAD

── LINE OF ALTERNATING BRONZE AND SILVER 11/0 SEED BEADS

|||| BRONZE #2 BUGLE BEADS

● FILL WITH IRIS SMOKE MATTE 11/0 SEED BEADS

– – LINE OF SILVER 11/0 SEED BEADS

Beaded Rainbow Vest

MATERIALS

One purchased lace vest
86 aqua 15-mm bugle beads
672 aqua #2 bugle beads

956 AB finished light sapphire 9/0 two-cut beads
229 lustered red 6/0 seed beads
229 lustered lilac 11/0 seed beads

DIRECTIONS

Stitch beads onto vest as desired; see General Instructions for "Sewing on Lace" on page 129.

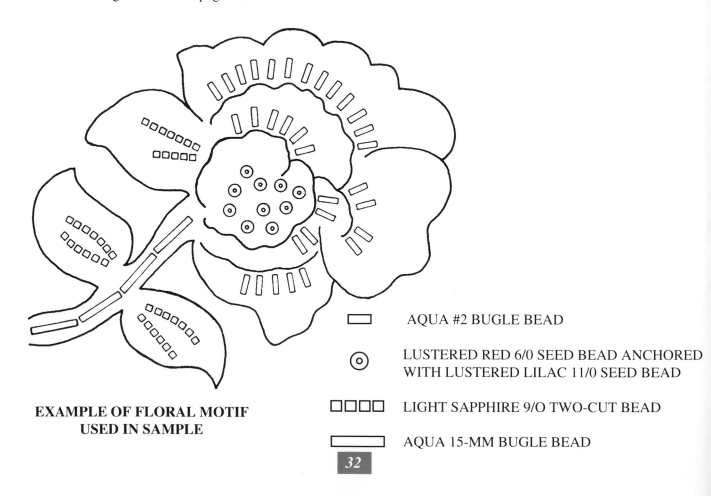

**EXAMPLE OF FLORAL MOTIF
USED IN SAMPLE**

▭ AQUA #2 BUGLE BEAD

◉ LUSTERED RED 6/0 SEED BEAD ANCHORED
   WITH LUSTERED LILAC 11/0 SEED BEAD

▭▭▭▭ LIGHT SAPPHIRE 9/O TWO-CUT BEAD

▭▭▭ AQUA 15-MM BUGLE BEAD

Cat Bag

MATERIALS

11/0 seed beads:
    3 oz. lustered white
    3 oz. lustered medium lavender
    3 oz. lustered pale lavender
    3 oz. dark blue-purple
    3 oz. metallic gold
    3 oz. light blue

20 iris matte green #2 bugle beads
8" x 10" piece of 14-count interlock needlepoint canvas
¼ yard of white satin fabric
¼ yard of stiff interfacing
1½ yards of ⅜" twisted satin cord
Two 1" x 2" strips of bronze or gold leather
Tracing paper
Tape

DIRECTIONS

All seams are ¼".

1. Stitch cat pattern on page 35 on needlepoint canvas. Trim canvas ½" from edge of design. Refer to General Instructions for "Sewing on Needlepoint Canvas" on page 130.

2. Using beaded piece as pattern, cut one cat from interfacing. From satin, cut three cats and four 1¼" x 2" strips. From satin cord, cut two 28" lengths.

3. With wrong sides facing and turning all edges under ¼", hand-stitch one satin cat piece to beaded front.

4. Layer interfacing and two satin pieces with right sides facing. Stitch, aligning edges and leaving a small opening in side seam; turn. Whipstitch closed.

5. To make purse loops, fold one long edge of one 1¼" x 2" satin strip under ¼"; press. Threefold long edges, starting with raw edge and ending with folded edge; topstitch. With right sides facing, stitch short ends together; turn. Repeat with remaining satin strips. Stitch each loop to inside of bag; see diagram.

6. With wrong sides facing, hand-stitch beaded front to back, starting one-third from top on side, around bottom and up to one-third from top on the other side.

7. Thread satin cording through the purse loops; see diagram. Stitch ends together, covering with tape. Using leather strips, cover taped joints; stitch; see diagram.

CAT BAG PATTERN

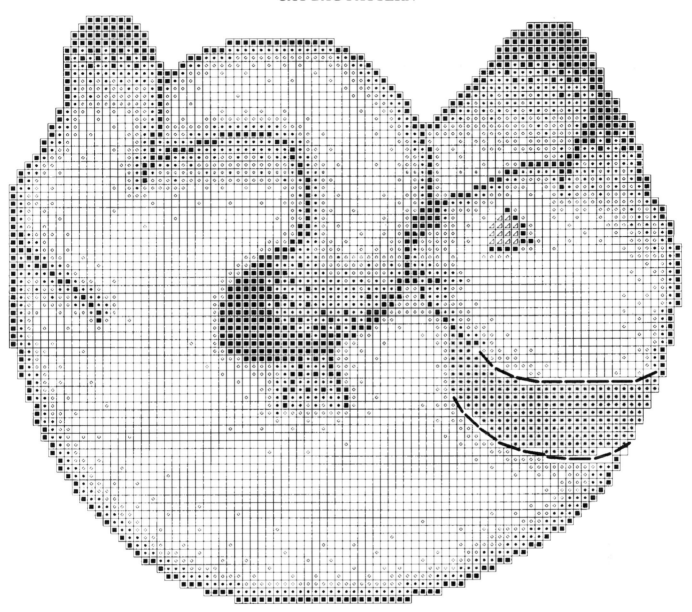

■ DARK BLUE-PURPLE 11/0 SEED BEAD
⊡ LUSTERED MEDIUM LAVENDER 11/0 SEED BEAD
◇ LUSTERED PALE LAVENDER 11/0 SEED BEAD
☐ LUSTERED WHITE 11/0 SEED BEAD
✳ METALLIC GOLD 11/0 SEED BEAD
◺ LIGHT BLUE 11/0 SEED BEAD

▮ IRIS MATTE GREEN #2 BUGLE BEAD

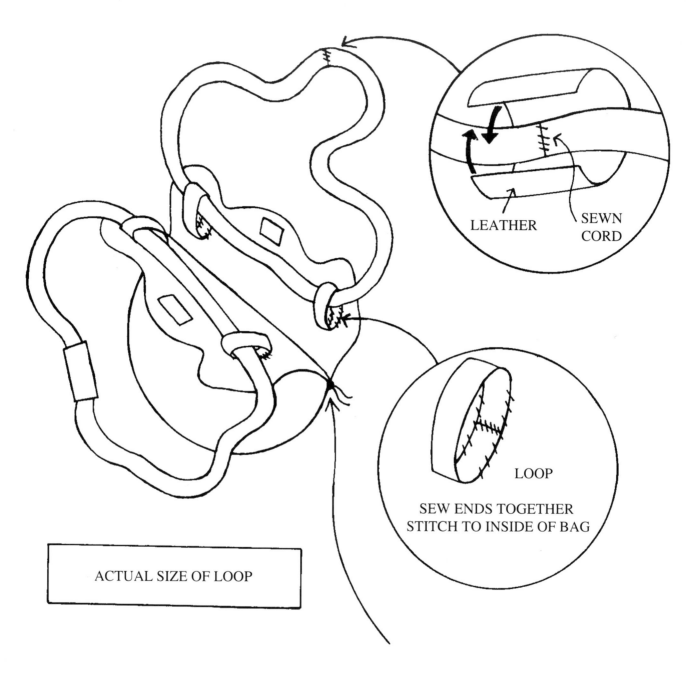

LEATHER

SEWN CORD

LOOP

SEW ENDS TOGETHER
STITCH TO INSIDE OF BAG

ACTUAL SIZE OF LOOP

DIAGRAM

Red Floral Earrings

MATERIALS

58 lustered red 6/0 seed beads
30 transparent amethyst 8/0 seed beads
80 AB finished transparent blue 9/0 two-cut beads
60 lustered orchid 11/0 seed beads
10 matte turquoise #5 bugle beads

Two turquoise 8-mm discs
Bead card
Earring posts
Scrap of fabric
Fusible webbing
Glue

DIRECTIONS

1. Transfer earring pattern to bead card. Stitch turquoise disc anchored with an orchid 11/0 seed bead at center of bead card. Continue beading according to pattern.

2. Using beaded design as pattern, cut one fabric backing piece for each earring. Apply fusible webbing to wrong side of fabric. Fuse fabric to wrong side of beadwork; see General Instructions for "Fusible Webbing" on page 126. Trim.

3. Glue earring posts to fabric.

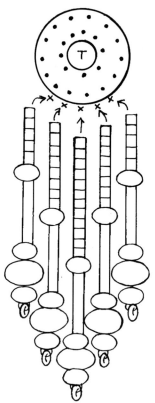

RED FLORAL EARRING PATTERN

● LUSTERED RED 6/0 SEED BEAD ANCHORED WITH LUSTERED ORCHID 11/0 SEED BEAD

Ⓣ TURQUOISE 8-MM DISK ANCHORED WITH LUSTERED ORCHID 11/0 SEED BEAD

⬭ TRANSPARENT AMETHYST 8/0 SEED BEAD

⬮ LUSTERED RED 6/0 SEED BEAD

▢ AB FINISHED TRANSPARENT BLUE 9/0 TWO-CUT BEAD

▯ MATTE TURQUOISE #5 BUGLE BEAD

⬭ LUSTERED ORCHID 11/0 SEED BEAD

✕ ATTACH FRINGES HERE

Bridal Pearl Necklace

MATERIALS

200 3-mm freshwater pearls
200 satin-finished peach 12/0 three-cut beads
Two AB finished 6-mm crystals with large holes
#0 nylon thread

One necklace clasp set
One very fine beading needle
Glue

DIRECTIONS

1. Beginning 4" from end of nylon thread length, thread one 12/0 bead, one pearl; repeat until there are 63 pearls on the thread, end with one 12/0 bead. Cut, leaving a 4" tail. Repeat, making two more strands.

2. Handling three strands as one, tie a knot at each end closely against beads. Glue.

3. While glue is still wet, thread glued end through the crystal, then through the loop at one end of the clasp set. Pass back through the crystal, then through knot, back down into the last peach bead and last pearl. Pull tightly; clip. Twist all strands as one. Repeat for other end; see diagram.

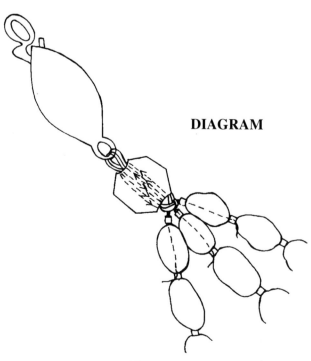

DIAGRAM

Bridal Drop Earrings

MATERIALS

Six .21 gauge gold finished 2½" headpins
Six 5-mm freshwater pearls
200 satin-finished peach 12/0 three-cut beads

Two jump rings
Purchased pearl stud earrings
Needle-nose pliers

DIRECTIONS

1. Cut two headpins 2¼" long, two 2" long and two 1¾" long.

2. Slide one freshwater pearl to the end of each headpin. Slide 12/0 three-cut beads onto each headpin, leaving ⅜" space remaining at end.

3. Using needle-nose pliers, make a loop at end of each headpin. Attach one headpin of each length to jump ring, arranging in order of length from shortest to longest. Close loops on all headpins. Bend each beaded headpin slightly; see diagram.

4. To wear, slip jump ring over the post of earring stud. Insert through ear.

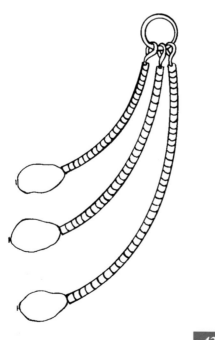

DIAGRAM

Bridal Purse

MATERIALS

1 yard of white satin fabric
⅛ yard of peach satin fabric
¼ yard of white organdy fabric
¼ yard of medium-weight white felt
1" of thin elastic cord
One lace appliqué
3 oz. of lustered white 11/0 seed beads

Nine satin-finished white #3 bugle beads
Three 6-mm crystals
13 freshwater pearls
120 satin-finished peach 12/0 three-cut beads
Tracing paper
Thread

DIRECTIONS

All seams are ½".

1. Make patterns on pages 45 and 46, transferring all information. From organdy, cut one front overlay piece and one flap piece. From peach satin, cut one flap piece. From felt, cut one flap piece and one front and one back piece. From white satin, cut one flap piece and two front and two back pieces. Also from white satin, cut 1"-wide bias strips, piecing as needed to equal 1 yard.

2. To embellish flap, stitch lace to right side of organdy flap; see photo. Stitch beads as desired; refer to General Instructions for "Sewing on Lace" on page 129.

3. To make front overlay, gather top and bottom edges of organdy, pulling in to match the size and shape of white satin front piece; see pattern. Begin layering front pieces as follows: right side up, organdy, satin, felt, and wrong side satin; see Diagram A. Baste. Cut one 8" length from bias strip. With right sides facing, stitch bias strip to top of organdy-covered front piece. Fold to wrong side, turning under ¼". Whipstitch in place; see Diagram B. Set front aside.

4. Layer back and flap pieces as follows: white satin flap right side down, white satin back right side up, felt back, white satin back right side down, organdy flap right side up, peach satin flap right side up, and felt flap. Stitch layers together along top edge; see Diagram C. Trim edge and press open. Baste; see Diagram D.

5. With wrong sides facing, baste front to back. Trim closely to stitch edge. With right sides facing, stitch bias strip to purse, rounding corner; see Diagram E. Fold to wrong side, turning under ¼". Whipstitch in place.

6. To make closure, fold elastic cord in half and stitch under lace at "V" of front flap. Stitch 6-mm crystal bead in place; see Diagram E.

7. To make handle, cut four 20" lengths of thread. Thread beads onto each length. Handling all four as one; twist. Thread one 6-mm crystal bead to each end. Stitch to each corner of back flap seam; see Diagram F.

DIAGRAM A

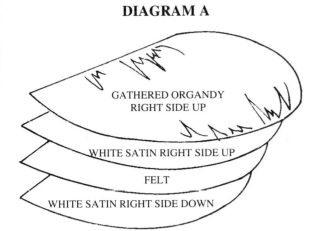

GATHERED ORGANDY
RIGHT SIDE UP

WHITE SATIN RIGHT SIDE UP

FELT

WHITE SATIN RIGHT SIDE DOWN

DIAGRAM B

8" BIAS STRIP

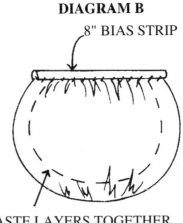

BASTE LAYERS TOGETHER

DIAGRAM C

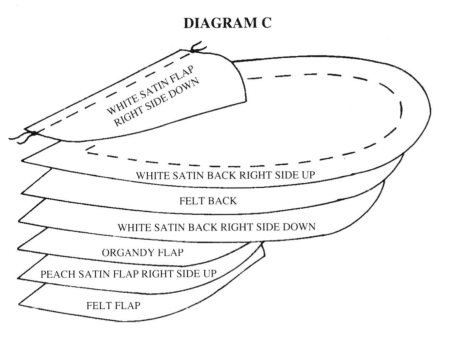

WHITE SATIN FLAP
RIGHT SIDE DOWN

WHITE SATIN BACK RIGHT SIDE UP

FELT BACK

WHITE SATIN BACK RIGHT SIDE DOWN

ORGANDY FLAP

PEACH SATIN FLAP RIGHT SIDE UP

FELT FLAP

DIAGRAM D

PRESSED TRIMMED SEAM

BASTE LAYERS TOGETHER

DIAGRAM E

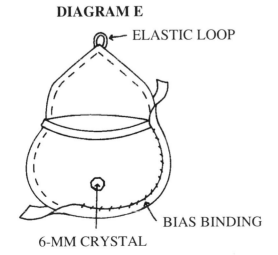

ELASTIC LOOP

6-MM CRYSTAL

BIAS BINDING

DIAGRAM F

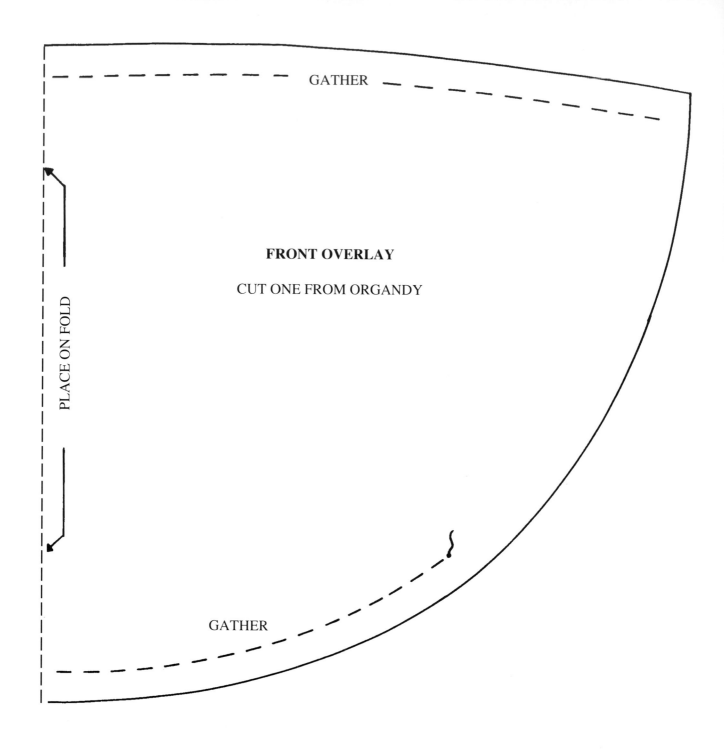

GATHER

FRONT OVERLAY

CUT ONE FROM ORGANDY

PLACE ON FOLD

GATHER

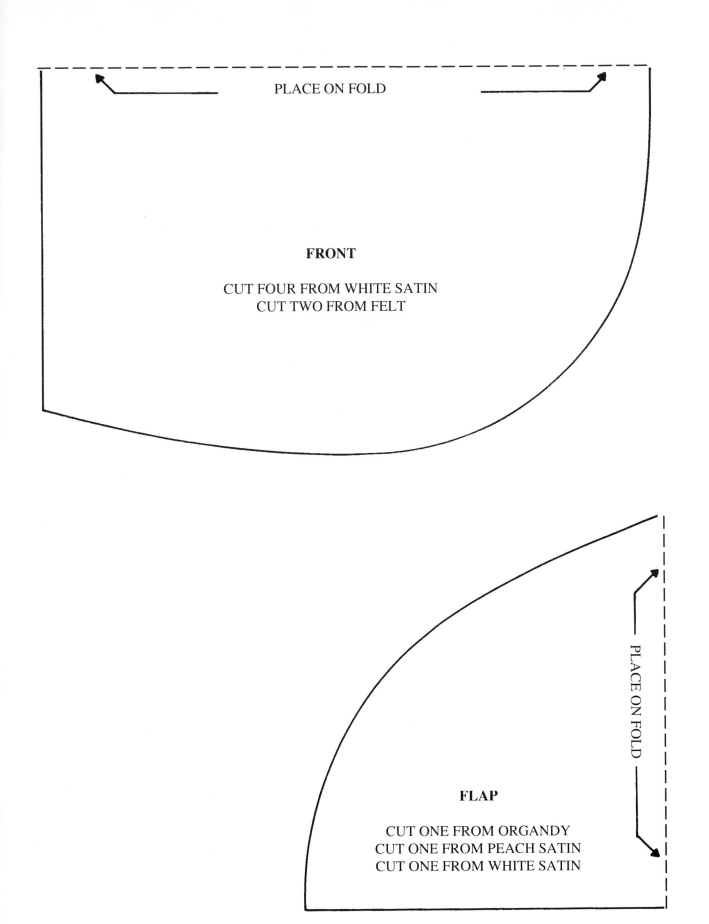

PLACE ON FOLD

FRONT

CUT FOUR FROM WHITE SATIN
CUT TWO FROM FELT

FLAP

CUT ONE FROM ORGANDY
CUT ONE FROM PEACH SATIN
CUT ONE FROM WHITE SATIN

PLACE ON FOLD

Bridal Gown

MATERIALS

One purchased bridal gown
9 oz. of satin-finished peach 12/0 three-cut beads
12 oz. of lustered satin-finished white 11/0 seed beads
9 oz. of satin-finished white #3 bugle beads
Four 16" strands of 3-mm freshwater pearls

16 AB finished 4-mm crystal beads
Eight 10-mm faux pearl wrist closures
Thread

DIRECTIONS

Bead as desired. Refer to General Instructions for
"Sewing on Lace" on page 129.

☐ SATIN-FINISHED PEACH 12/0 THREE-CUT BEAD

▭ SATIN-FINISHED WHITE #3 BUGLE BEAD

○ LUSTERED SATIN-FINISHED WHITE 11/0 SEED BEAD

◯ 3-MM FRESHWATER PEARL

⬡ AB FINISHED 4-MM CRYSTAL BEAD

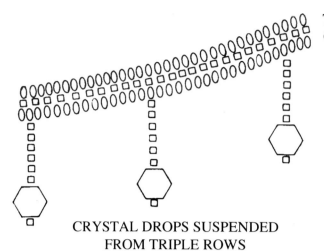

TRIPLE ROW OF BEADS
COVERS EMPIRE SEAM

CRYSTAL DROPS SUSPENDED
FROM TRIPLE ROWS

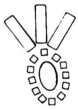

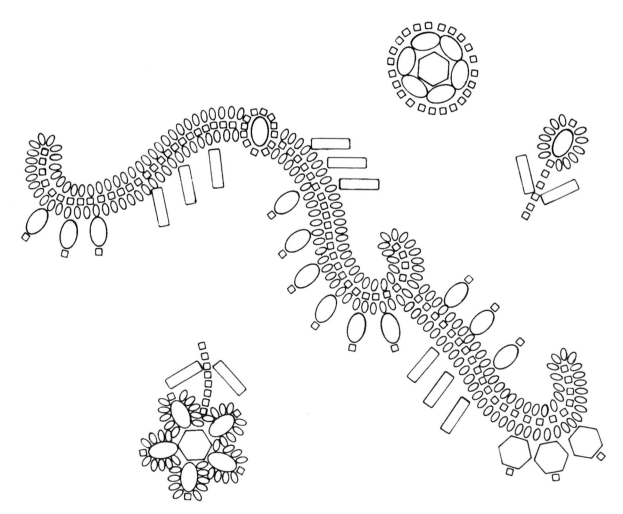

**EXAMPLE OF BEADED MOTIF
USED ON SAMPLE**

Butterfly Camisole

MATERIALS

One purchased camisole
Scrap of metallic silver fabric
Scrap of fusible webbing
3 oz. of silver-lined crystal 11/0 seed beads
1 oz. of rainbow-lined 11/0 seed beads
1 oz. of iris purple 12/0 three-cut beads

30 5-mm freshwater pearls
50 AB finished crystal 6/0 seed beads
Four AB finished crystal smoky 6-mm beads
1 oz. of silver-lined crystal #2 bugle beads
Tracing paper

DIRECTIONS

1. Transfer pattern on page 53 onto camisole. Fuse webbing to wrong side of metallic fabric. Cut one butterfly body from fused fabric. Fuse body to camisole. Refer to General Instructions for "Fusing" on page 126.

2. Stitch beads on camisole according to pattern.

3. Attach fringe to center bottom of butterfly body; see pattern.

LINES OF SILVER-LINED CRYSTAL 11/0 SEED BEADS; BACKTRACK

LINES OF IRIS PURPLE 12/0 THREE-CUT BEADS

LINES OF RAINBOW-LINED 11/0 SEED BEADS

5-MM FRESHWATER PEARL

AB FINISHED CRYSTAL SMOKY 6-MM BEAD

AB FINISHED CRYSTAL 6/0 SEED BEAD

INDIVIDUAL SILVER-LINED CRYSTAL 11/0 SEED BEADS

SILVER-LINED CRYSTAL #2 BUGLE BEAD

M   FILL WITH RAINBOW-LINED 11/0 SEED BEAD

SILVER-LINED CRYSTAL 11/0
AB FINISHED CRYSTAL 6/0
FRESHWATER PEARL

TEMPLATE FOR
BUTTERFLY BODY

BUTTERFLY CAMISOLE
PATTERN

Turquoise Purse Flap

MATERIALS

One purchased fabric purse with top edge 6"–7" wide
5" x 9" piece of gray felt
120 iris purple matte 6/0 seed beads
One 13-mm x 18-mm gemstone cabochon
180 turquoise matte #5 bugles beads
Eight root beer #2 bugle beads
160 copper 11/0 seed beads

80 bronze 11/0 seed beads
Two jagged ¼"-diameter turquoise chunk
Two smooth ¼"-diameter turquoise chunk
One turquoise 30-mm donut bead
10 yards of silver rayon floss
Gray thread
Glue

DIRECTIONS

1. Transfer pattern on page 56 to felt. Bead according to pattern.

2. Fill in upper and lower areas with turquoise #5 bugle beads. Sew lines of iris purple 6/0 seed beads anchored with copper 11/0 seed beads. Sew turquoise chunks in center.

3. Sew individual iris purple 6/0 seed beads anchored with copper 11/0 seed beads and root beer bugle beads in center area. Glue cabochon in oval in center.

4. Outline with lines of copper and bronze 11/0 seed beads.

5. Hand-stitch beaded felt to front flap of purse.

6. Sew 12"-long strands of floss to triangular area in the lower center of the flap until desired tassel weight is achieved. Handling bundle as one, pull through donut hole; tie large knot. Push floss ends back through the donut hole and trim to 6"; see diagram.

TURQUOISE PURSE FLAP PATTERN

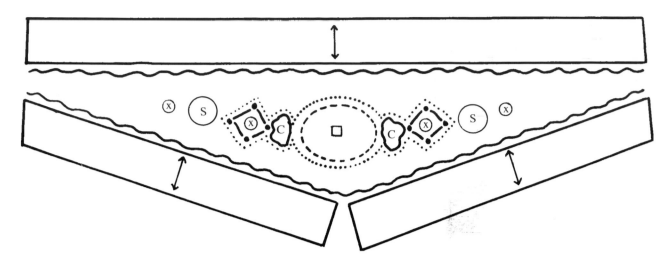

$\updownarrow$ FILL WITH TURQUOISE MATTE #5 BUGLE BEADS IN THE DIRECTION OF THE ARROWS

□ 13-MM X 18-MM GEMSTONE CABOCHON

Ⓧ IRIS PURPLE MATTE 6/0 SEED BEAD ANCHORED WITH COPPER 11/0 SEED BEAD

Ⓒ JAGGED TURQUOISE CHUNK

Ⓢ SMOOTH TURQUOISE CHUNK

—— ROOT BEER #2 BUGLE BEAD

• INDIVIDUAL COPPER 11/0 SEED BEAD

– – LINES OF COPPER 11/0 SEED BEADS

····· LINES OF BRONZE 11/0 SEED BEADS

DIAGRAM

Turquoise Belt

MATERIALS

One 2¼"-wide purchased belt with back closure
Scraps of deep purple suede or ultrasuede
Scraps of lavender and emerald leather
11/0 seed beads:
    1 oz. light topaz matte
    1 oz. lavender matte
    1 oz. turquoise matte
    28 green matte
6/0 seed beads:
    28 topaz matte
    22 iris purple matte

80 metallic gold 12/0 three-cut beads
Three turquoise 12-mm discs
Six turquoise chunks
Four cape amethyst chips
Two turquoise matte #5 bugle beads
Fusible webbing
Tracing paper
Leather glue

DIRECTIONS

1. Make templates on page 59. Adhere fusible webbing to back of leather and suede scraps; refer to General Instructions for "Fusing" on page 126. Cut templates.

2. Layer purple suede on lavender and green leather inside dashed line; see Diagram A. Fuse in place.

3. Stitch beads onto leather; see Diagram A.

4. Glue beaded leather to belt; see Diagram B.

⎯⎯ OUTLINE WITH TURQUOISE MATTE 11/0 SEED BEADS; BACKTRACK

• METALLIC GOLD 12/0 THREE-CUT BEAD

◯ IRIS PURPLE MATTE 6/0 SEED BEAD ANCHORED WITH METALLIC GOLD 12/0 THREE-CUT BEAD

⊙ LIGHT TOPAZ MATTE 11/0 SEED BEAD ANCHORED WITH GREEN MATTE 11/0 SEED BEAD

Ⓐ CAPE AMETHYST CHIP

Ⓣ TURQUOISE CHUNK

- - - - OUTLINE WITH TOPAZ MATTE 11/0 SEED BEADS

○ TOPAZ MATTE 6/0 SEED BEAD

· · · · LINE OF METALLIC GOLD 12/0 THREE-CUT BEADS

⊬ TURQUOISE MATTE #5 BUGLE BEAD

Ⓓ TURQUOISE DISC ANCHORED WITH METALLIC GOLD 12/0 THREE-CUT BEAD

•⎯• OUTLINE WITH LAVENDER MATTE 11/0 SEED BEADS; BACKTRACK

TEMPLATES

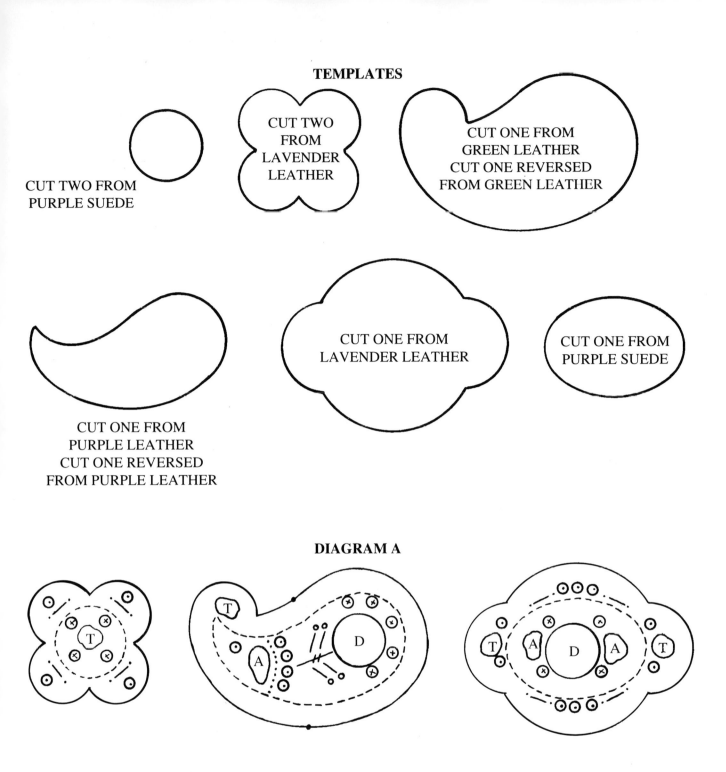

CUT TWO FROM
PURPLE SUEDE

CUT TWO
FROM
LAVENDER
LEATHER

CUT ONE FROM
GREEN LEATHER
CUT ONE REVERSED
FROM GREEN LEATHER

CUT ONE FROM
PURPLE LEATHER
CUT ONE REVERSED
FROM PURPLE LEATHER

CUT ONE FROM
LAVENDER LEATHER

CUT ONE FROM
PURPLE SUEDE

DIAGRAM A

DIAGRAM B

Fish Eyeglass Case

MATERIALS

11/0 seed beads:
   1 oz. lustered aqua
   1 oz. lustered medium purple
   1 oz. lustered medium green
   1 oz. lustered yellow
   1 oz. lustered pale peach
   1 oz. lustered royal blue
   1 oz. lustered lavender
   1 oz. lustered pale pink
   1 oz. lustered tangerine
   1 oz. opaque coral
   1 oz. iris blue

66 pink #2 bugle beads
16 light green #2 bugle beads
One iris blue 4-mm round bead
5" x 8" piece of 14-count needlepoint canvas
¼ yard of black satin fabric
¼ yard of stiff interfacing
24" length of ⅜" metallic gold cord
Two gold end caps
Tracing paper
Thread
Glue

DIRECTIONS

All seams are ¼".

1. Stitch fish pattern on page 62 on needlepoint canvas. Trim canvas to pattern. Refer to General Instructions for "Sewing on Needlepoint Canvas" on page 130.

2. Using beaded fish piece as pattern, cut three fishes from satin, adding ¼" to all edges. Cut one fish from interfacing.

3. With wrong sides facing and turning edges under ¼" all around, hand-stitch one satin piece to beaded front.

4. Layer interfacing and two satin pieces with right sides facing. Stitch, aligning edges, leaving small opening in side; turn. Whipstitch closed. With wrong sides facing, hand-stitch beaded front to back, leaving top edge open.

5. To make handle, glue ends of cord to keep from fraying; insert ends into end caps. Stitch caps to top corners of finished case.

▤	LUSTERED AQUA 11/0 SEED BEAD	⊡	LUSTERED PALE PINK 11/0 SEED BEAD
▣	LUSTERED MEDIUM PURPLE 11/0 SEED BEAD	⊞	LUSTERED TANGERINE 11/0 SEED BEAD
▣	LUSTERED MEDIUM GREEN 11/0 SEED BEAD	▣	OPAQUE CORAL 11/0 SEED BEAD
⊡	LUSTERED YELLOW 11/0 SEED BEAD	▣	IRIS BLUE 11/0 SEED BEAD
▣	LUSTERED PALE PEACH 11/0 SEED BEAD	❙	PINK #2 BUGLE BEADS
▣	LUSTERED ROYAL BLUE 11/0 SEED BEAD	❙	LIGHT GREEN #2 BUGLE BEADS
▣	LUSTERED LAVENDER 11/0 SEED BEAD	●	IRIS BLUE 4-MM ROUND BEAD

FISH EYEGLASS CASE PATTERN

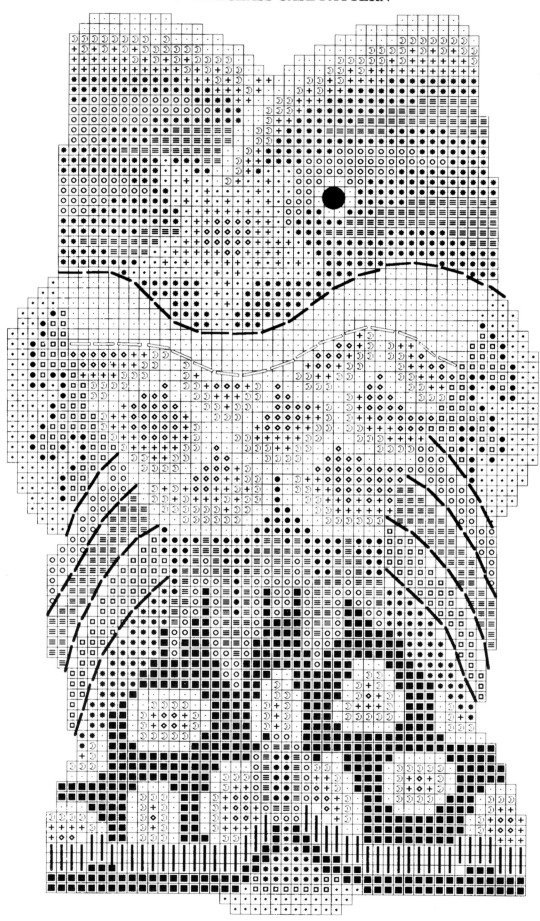

Paisley Bag

MATERIALS

11/0 seed beads:
   3 oz. opaque light green
   3 oz. opaque white
   3 oz. opaque red
   3 oz. opaque medium turquoise
   3 oz. opaque orange
   3 oz. opaque dark green
   3 oz. opaque pale aqua
   3 oz. opaque dark blue
   3 oz. opaque rose
   3 oz. opaque yellow
   3 oz. opaque black
   3 oz. opaque light blue-lavender

9" x 11" piece of 14-count interlock needlepoint canvas
¼ yard of black satin fabric; matching thread
¼ yard of black velvet fabric
One skein of natural candlewick cotton
Thread
Tracing paper

DIRECTIONS

All seams are ¼".

1. Stitch paisley pattern on pages 66–69 on needlepoint canvas. Trim canvas to one row larger than pattern along bottom edge only. Refer to General Instructions for "Sewing on Needlepoint Canvas" on page 130.

2. Using beaded design as pattern, cut two pieces from satin, adding ¼" to all edges. Cut one piece from velvet, adding ¼" to all edges.

3. With right sides facing and turning edges under ¼" all around, hand-stitch one satin piece to beaded front, leaving one row of needlepoint canvas exposed at bottom.

4. With right sides facing and edges aligned, stitch one satin and one velvet piece together, leaving small opening in side seam. Turn; whipstitch closed. With satin pieces facing, hand-stitch back to front, leaving top edge open.

5. To make fringe, cut 184 strands of candlewick cotton 8" long. Starting at bottom center and handling eight strands of cotton as one, thread through needlepoint canvas and knot; see Diagram A. Continue working out towards each side until complete. Trim fringe to 2½".

6. To make handle, cut 150 strands of candlewick cotton 2 yards long. Divide strands into thirds and make a 30"-long braid. Tie a knot in each end, leaving a 2" fringe. Repeat to make other handle. Attach handles to bag, stitching through each knot; see Diagram B.

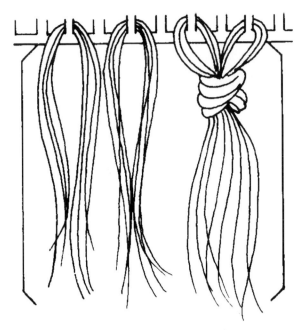

DIAGRAM A

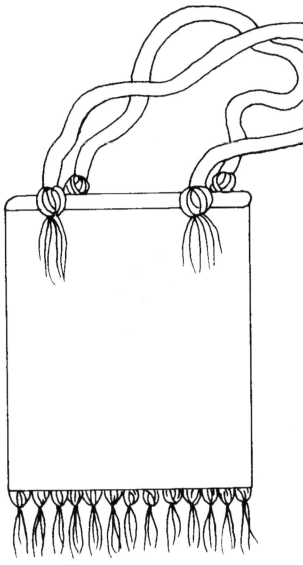

DIAGRAM B

⊡ OPAQUE LIGHT GREEN 11/0 SEED BEAD

◎ OPAQUE ORANGE 11/0 SEED BEAD

✳ OPAQUE ROSE 111/0 SEED BEAD

☐ OPAQUE WHITE 11/0 SEED BEAD

◙ OPAQUE DARK GREEN 11/0 SEED BEAD

⊙ OPAQUE YELLOW 11/0 SEED BEAD

☒ OPAQUE RED 11/0 SEED BEAD

⊞ OPAQUE PALE AQUA 11/0 SEED BEAD

■ OPAQUE BLACK 11/0 SEED BEAD

◈ OPAQUE MEDIUM TURQUOISE 11/0 SEED BEAD

▦ OPAQUE DARK BLUE 11/0 SEED BEAD

⊡ OPAQUE LIGHT BLUE-LAVENDER 11/0 SEED BEAD

PAISLEY BAG PATTERN

$\mathcal{S}$almon Coat & Pillbox Hat

MATERIALS

One purchased salmon coat
One purchased salmon 7"-diameter pillbox hat with
   2⅝" brim; see diagram

10/0 opaque seed beads:
   1 oz. pink
   1 oz. yellow
   1 oz. light green
   1 oz. light blue
   1 oz. black
   1 oz. aqua
   1 oz. brown

DIRECTIONS

Using patterns on pages 72 and 73, stitch beads as
desired; see photo.

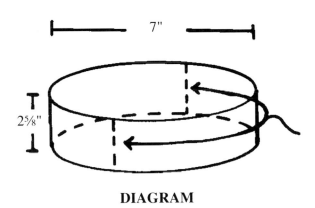

DIAGRAM

SALMON PILLBOX HAT PATTERN

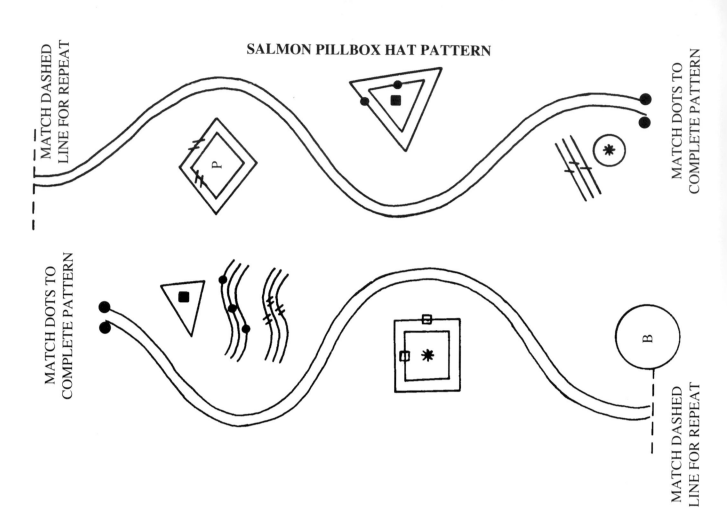

B   FILL WITH LIGHT BLUE OPAQUE 10/0 SEED BEADS

P   FILL WITH PINK OPAQUE 10/0 SEED BEADS

LINES OF AQUA OPAQUE 10/0 SEED BEADS

FILL WITH BLACK OPAQUE 10/0 SEED BEADS

LINES OF LIGHT BLUE OPAQUE 10/0 SEED BEADS

* FILL WITH BROWN OPAQUE 10/0 SEED BEADS

LINES OF LIGHT GREEN OPAQUE 10/0 SEED BEADS

DOUBLE LINES OF YELLOW OPAQUE 10/0 SEED BEADS

LINES OF PINK OPAQUE 10/0 SEED BEADS

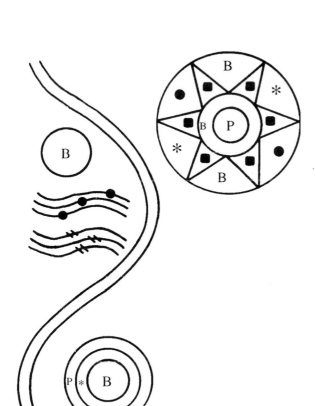

SALMON COAT PATTERN

B	FILL WITH LIGHT BLUE OPAQUE 10/0 SEED BEADS
P	FILL WITH PINK OPAQUE 10/0 SEED BEADS
⊬	LINES OF AQUA OPAQUE 10/0 SEED BEADS
■	FILL WITH BLACK OPAQUE 10/0 SEED BEADS
⊬	LINES OF LIGHT BLUE OPAQUE 10/0 SEED BEADS
*	FILL WITH BROWN OPAQUE 10/0 SEED BEADS
●—	LINES OF LIGHT GREEN OPAQUE 10/0 SEED BEADS
≈	DOUBLE LINES OF YELLOW OPAQUE 10/0 SEED BEADS
●	FILL WITH LIGHT GREEN OPAQUE 10/0 SEED BEADS

*B*lack Lace Collar

MATERIALS

Purchased black lace collar; matching thread
3 oz. of jet black 12/0 three-cut beads
3 oz. of lustered gray 12/0 three-cut beads
3 oz. of jet black #2 bugle beads

50 jet black English-cut crystals
One long smoky bi-cone crystal for fringe
Ten smoky 6-mm crystals
Two jet black 12-mm crystals

DIRECTIONS

Stitch beads onto collar as desired; see General Instructions for "Sewing on Lace" on page 129.

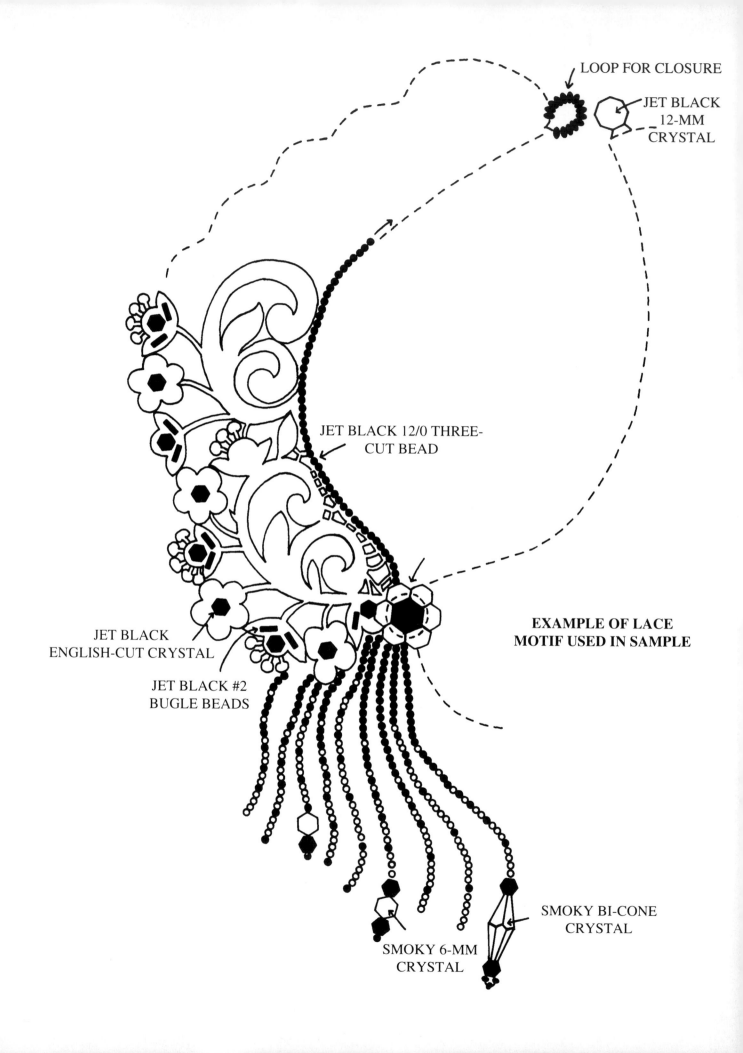

LOOP FOR CLOSURE

JET BLACK 12-MM CRYSTAL

JET BLACK 12/0 THREE-CUT BEAD

EXAMPLE OF LACE MOTIF USED IN SAMPLE

JET BLACK ENGLISH-CUT CRYSTAL

JET BLACK #2 BUGLE BEADS

SMOKY BI-CONE CRYSTAL

SMOKY 6-MM CRYSTAL

Teal Shawl

MATERIALS

1½ yards of teal lightweight rayon fabric
3 yards of 1½"-wide teal lace
One triangular teal lace panel

Thread
Assorted beads in complementary colors

DIRECTIONS

All seams are ½".

1. Pre-shrink rayon; press. Cut one 43" square.

2. With right sides facing, fold rayon in half along the diagonal. Stitch along raw edges, leaving small opening in side. Turn and press flat; see Diagram A. Whipstitch opening closed.

3. Stitch lace to rayon along all edges except folded edge. Stitch lace panel to bottom of shawl "V"; see Diagram B.

4. Embellish shawl with beads as desired; refer to General Instructions for "Sewing on Lace" on page 129.

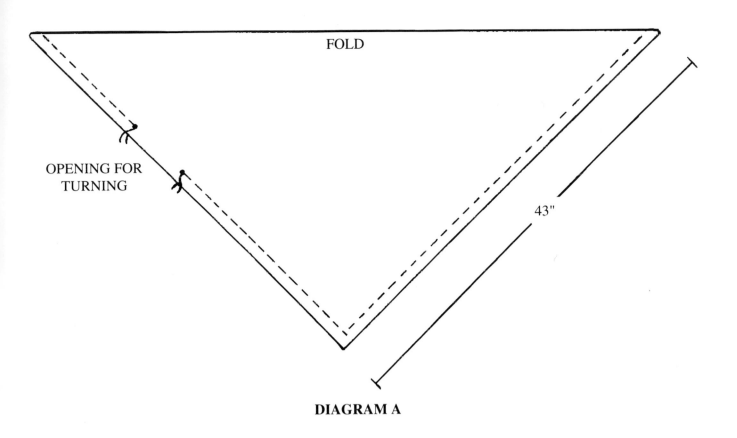

FOLD

OPENING FOR
TURNING

43"

DIAGRAM A

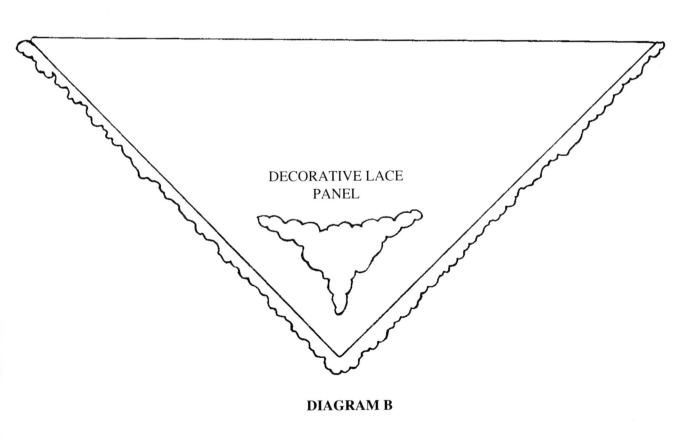

DECORATIVE LACE
PANEL

DIAGRAM B

Ginger Jar Bag

MATERIALS

11/0 seed beads
  3 oz. yellow
  3 oz. orange
  3 oz. bright coral
  3 oz. medium green
  3 oz. dark blue-purple
  3 oz. medium orchid
  3 oz. pink
  3 oz. iris blue
  3 oz. pale orange
  3 oz. medium lavender
  3 oz. aqua
  3 oz. light blue
  3 oz. dark orchid
  3 oz. pale orchid
  3 oz. metallic gold

9" x 11" piece of 14-count interlock needlepoint canvas
9" x 11" piece of gold-finished leather
¼ yard of lining fabric
¾ yard of ⅛" gold cord
2 yards of ¼" gold cord
Metallic gold thread

DIRECTIONS

1. Using needlepoint canvas, stitch pattern on page 83. Trim canvas to pattern. Refer to General Instructions for "Sewing on Needlepoint Canvas" on page 130.

2. Using beaded design as pattern, cut two from lining, adding ¼" to all edges. Cut one from leather for back, adding ¼" to all edges. Cut two 11" lengths from ⅛" cording.

3. With wrong sides facing, hand-stitch lining to beaded front, turning edges under ¼" all around. Repeat, stitching remaining lining piece to leather back.

4. With lining facing, hand-stitch front to back, leaving one-third from top edge open.

5. Using ⅛" cording, hand-stitch to edges on open third of top edge of bag.

6. Using ¼" cording, start at center bottom and hand-stitch one end two-thirds up one side of bag. Repeat, using other end of cord; see Diagram A.

7. Using metallic gold thread, make tassels to cover cord joint; see Diagram B.

⊡	ORANGE 11/0 SEED BEAD
⊠	PALE ORCHID 11/0 SEED BEAD
⊙	MEDIUM ORCHID 11/0 SEED BEAD
⊡	AQUA 11/0 SEED BEAD
◎	BRIGHT CORAL 11/0 SEED BEAD
▲	DARK ORCHID 11/0 SEED BEAD
▦	MEDIUM GREEN 11/0 SEED BEAD
◉	DARK BLUE-PURPLE 11/0 SEED BEAD
◼	IRIS BLUE 11/0 SEED BEAD
☐	YELLOW 11/0 SEED BEAD
⊡	PALE ORANGE 11/0 SEED BEAD
⊞	METALLIC GOLD 11/0 SEED BEAD
⊠	MEDIUM LAVENDER 11/0 SEED BEAD
⊞	PINK 11/0 SEED BEAD
⊡	LIGHT BLUE 11/0 SEED BEAD

DIAGRAM A

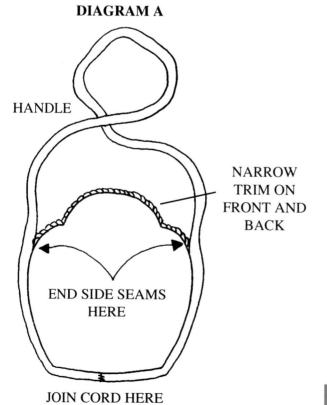

HANDLE

NARROW
TRIM ON
FRONT AND
BACK

END SIDE SEAMS
HERE

JOIN CORD HERE

DIAGRAM B

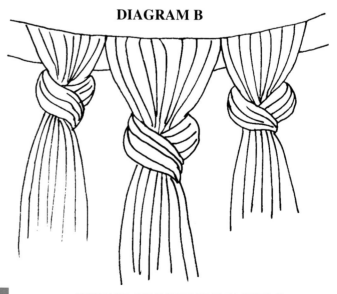

82

DETAIL OF BOTTOM TASSELS

THIS PATTERN SHOWS THE LEFT
HALF OF THE DESIGN. REPEAT IN
MIRROR IMAGE FOR RIGHT SIDE
(DO NOT REPEAT CENTER ROW)

FILL THIS SPACE WITH VERTICAL
SAPPHIRE SILVER-LINED #2 BUGLE
BEADS

END SIDE SEAMS HERE

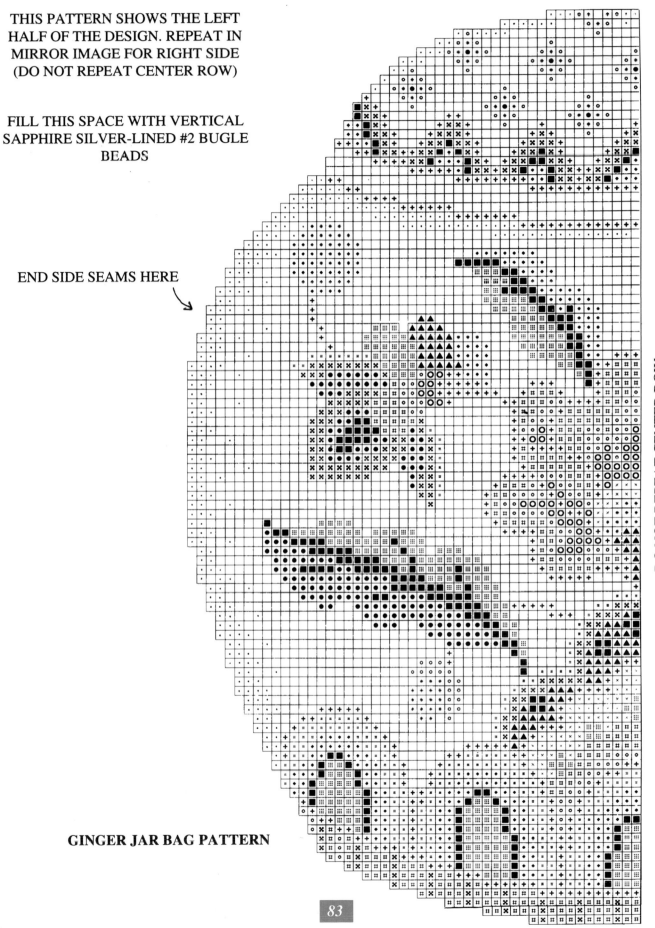

GINGER JAR BAG PATTERN

DO NOT REPEAT CENTER ROW

Chapter Two

Turquoise Button Earrings

MATERIALS

Two decorative silver buttons, approximately
   1" diameter
110 iris purple matte delica beads
116 aqua matte delica beads
316 metallic silver 12/0 three-cut beads
Six matte aqua #5 bugle beads

Six turquoise 10-mm tubes
114 iris purple 8/0 seed beads
Ten iris purple 5-mm teardrops
Bead card
Two earring posts
Scraps of fabric for backing
Scraps of fusible webbing

DIRECTIONS

1. Transfer button pattern to bead card. Following solid line, outline bead card with metallic silver 12/0 three-cut beads; backtrack.

2. Sew iris purple 8/0 seed beads along dashed line. Glue button to card. Sew turquoise bead through button holes. Add fringes as diagrammed.

3. Attach backing to wrong side of bead card. Refer to General Instructions for "Fusing" on page 126.

4. Glue earring post to back of earring. Repeat Steps 1–4 to make other earring.

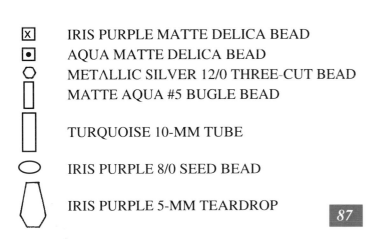

☒	IRIS PURPLE MATTE DELICA BEAD
⊡	AQUA MATTE DELICA BEAD
⬡	METALLIC SILVER 12/0 THREE-CUT BEAD
▯	MATTE AQUA #5 BUGLE BEAD
▯	TURQUOISE 10-MM TUBE
⬭	IRIS PURPLE 8/0 SEED BEAD
⬗	IRIS PURPLE 5-MM TEARDROP

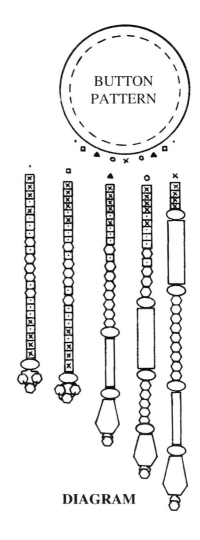

BUTTON PATTERN

DIAGRAM

ℬeaded Watch Band

MATERIALS

One watch face with spring clips
Five-hole band (compatible with watch face)
Bracelet clasp

#0 nylon thread
Assorted beads
Glue

DIRECTIONS

1. To find the size of watch band and amount of beads needed, measure wrist, minus the size of watch face, minus 1", then divide in half. Buy enough beads of choice to make six strands.

2. Cut six strands of nylon thread to size determined in Step 1, adding 3". Make beaded strands; see diagram. Thread ends through five-hole band; tie and glue. Thread other ends through clasp. Thread ends back through beads; tie and glue.

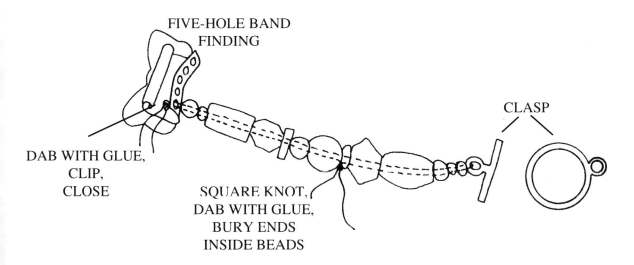

FIVE-HOLE BAND
FINDING

CLASP

DAB WITH GLUE,
CLIP,
CLOSE

SQUARE KNOT,
DAB WITH GLUE,
BURY ENDS
INSIDE BEADS

DIAGRAM

Queen of Bags

MATERIALS

For Queen's Face
11/0 seed beads:
- 3 oz. of white
- 3 oz. of pale lavender
- 3 oz. of lustered amethyst
- 3 oz. of beige
- 3 oz. of matte light topaz
- 3 oz. of transparent rainbow topaz
- 1 oz. of black
- 1 oz. of rose
- 1 oz. of red
- 1 oz. of medium blue lustered

For Crown
11/0 seed beads:
- 6 oz. lustered pale blue
- 1200 metallic gold
- 800 silver-lined dark amethyst

280 transparent amethyst 8/0 seed beads
88 gold metallic gold 6/0 seed beads
6 oz. silver-lined gold #2 bugle beads
Two 18-mm x 26-mm magenta acrylic cabochon
Four 12-mm square royal blue acrylic cabochon
Two 18-mm round emerald green acrylic cabochon
Eight AB finished pale blue 6-mm firepolished crystals
28 4-mm freshwater pearls
Two 4" x 7" pieces of lightweight leather for backing
Two 4" x 7" pieces of fusible webbing
Bead card
Thread
Glue

For Handle
1200 lustered pale blue 11/0 seed beads
120 silver-lined gold #2 bugle beads
Six 24" lengths of size 0 nylon thread
Two gold-finished end caps

DIRECTIONS

1. Weave queen pattern on page 94. Refer to General Instructions for "Needleweaving" on page 133. Make two faces. Set aside. *Hint: When threading on the top three beads in each row, make sure that they have clear holes. Sort through the beads of the color you are using in the top three beads to find those with the largest holes. You will be sewing the face to the crown through the holes of the top three beads, so there will be a heavy buildup of thread.*

2. Transfer crown pattern on page 93 to bead card; stitch two crowns. Refer to General Instructions for "Beading on Surfaces" on page 125. Stitch on all #2 bugle beads. Stitch on 8/0 seed beads, position acrylic cabochons inside outlined areas to check for fit, then glue the cabochons in place. Backtrack through 8/0 seed beads to secure the cabochons.

3. Stitch on freshwater pearls and crystals. Stitch on 6/0 seed beads, anchoring with 11/0 seed beads. Stitch lines of 11/0 seed beads, then backtrack. Fill in background with pale blue and silver-lined dark amethyst as indicated.

4. Using beaded crown piece as pattern, cut two each from leather and fusible webbing. Attach backing to wrong side of crown. Refer to General Instructions for "Fusing" on page 126.

5. Attach each face to each crown by weaving back and forth through the lower bugle beads of the crown and the top three beads in each row of the weaving; see diagram on page 93. *Note: there will be more bugle beads than rows of weave, skip bugle beads as needed.*

6. With wrong sides facing, stitch bag together from lower edge of crown, around the face to other lower edge of crown.

7. To make handle, using six 24" length of nylon thread, thread each length with beads as follows: 1 seed, 1 bugle, 1 seed, 1 bugle, 2 seed, 1 bugle, 3 seed, 1 bugle, 4 seed, 1 bugle, 5 seed, 1 bugle, 6 seed, 1 bugle, 7 seed, 1 bugle, 8 seed, 1 bugle, 8" of seed, 1 bugle, 8 seed, 1 bugle, 7 seed, 1 bugle, 6 seed, 1 bugle, 5 seed, 1 bugle, 4 seed, 1 bugle, 3 seed, 1 bugle, 2 seed, 1 bugle, 1 seed, 1 bugle, 1 seed. Repeat five more times. Handling six strands as one, thread through end cap; fasten off. Twist all six strands together, thread through other end cap, and fasten off. Attach handle end caps to top edges of crown.

DIAGRAM

CROWN PATTERN

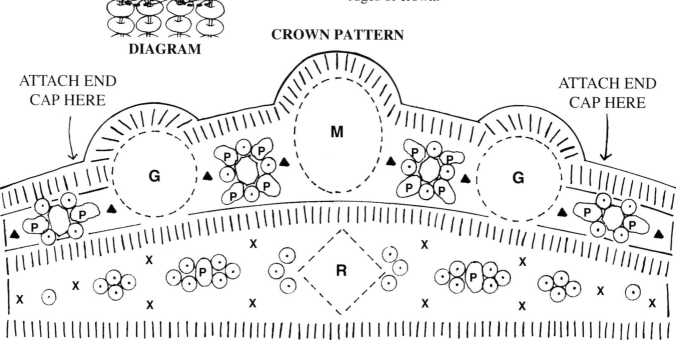

- - - - - OUTLINE WITH TRANSPARENT AMETHYST 8/0 SEED BEADS

—— INDIVIDUAL SILVER-LINED #2 BUGLE BEADS

〰〰 LINE OF METALLIC GOLD 11/0 SEED BEADS (BACKTRACK)

◯ AB FINISHED PALE BLUE 6-MM FIREPOLISHED CRYSTAL

M MAGENTA CABOCHON

G EMERALD GREEN CABOCHON

R ROYAL BLUE CABOCHON

Ⓟ 4-MM FRESHWATER PEARL

⊙ METALLIC GOLD 6/0 SEED BEAD ANCHORED WITH METALLIC GOLD 11/0

▲ FILL WITH SILVER-LINED DARK AMETHYST 11/0 SEED BEADS

X FILL WITH LUSTERED PALE BLUE 11/0 SEED BEADS

QUEEN OF BAGS PATTERN

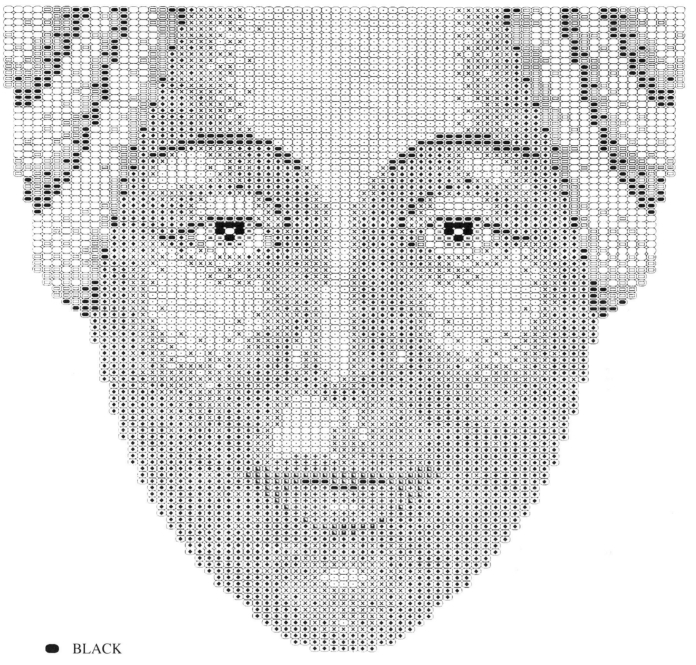

- ⬤ BLACK
- ◉ LUSTERED AMETHYST
- ⬭ PALE LAVENDER
- ⬭ WHITE
- ⊙ BEIGE
- ⊜ MEDIUM BLUE LUSTERED
- ⊗ MATTE LIGHT TOPAZ
- ◈ TRANSPARENT RAINBOW TOPAZ
- ⊡ RED
- ⊕ ROSE

Queen of Pins

MATERIALS

Delica beads:
  white
  dark beige
  cobalt blue
  off-white
  pink
  light blue
  red
  dark red
80 metallic gold 10/0 seed beads

100 metallic gold 12/0 three-cut beads
Five 6-mm crystals
One 8-mm crystal
Two 3-mm freshwater pearls
33 AB finished emerald green #2 bugle beads
25 metallic gold #2 bugle beads
16 transparent amethyst 8/0 seed beads
262 AB finished transparent amber 11/0 seed beads
Scrap of fabric for backing
Scrap of fusible webbing
One pinback

DIRECTIONS

1. Weave queen pattern on page 96. Refer to General Instructions for "Needleweaving" on page 133. Set aside.

2. Transfer crown pattern on page 95 to bead card. Sew beads to bead card following pattern. Refer to General Instructions for "Beading on Surfaces" on page 125. Do not sew transparent amber drapes until after the face is sewn onto the bottom of the crown.

3. Attach backing to wrong side of bead card. Refer to General Instructions for "Fusing" on page 126. Trim bead card, leaving ⅛" on lower edge of crown.

4. Sew woven design piece to stitched bead card using small invisible stitches.

5. Sew on drapes according to pattern. Sew six fringes of amber 11/0, each 34 beads long, under the right side drape. Refer to General Instructions for "Fringes" on page 139.

6. Sew on pinback.

QUEEN OF PINS PATTERN

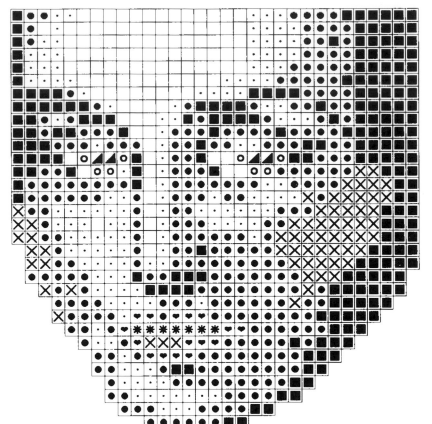

■	DARK BEIGE DELICA BEAD
✕	PINK DELICA BEAD
♥	RED DELICA BEAD
✳	DARK RED DELICA BEAD
◢	COBALT DELICA BEAD
⊙	LIGHT BLUE DELICA BEAD
·	OFF-WHITE DELICA BEAD
☐	WHITE DELICA BEAD

CROWN PATTERN

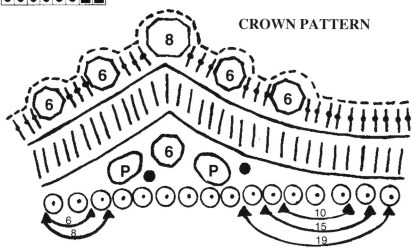

⊙	8/0 AMETHYST SEED BEAD ANCHORED WITH GOLD 12/0 THREE CUT
⑥	6-MM CRYSTAL
⑧	8-MM CRYSTAL
—	LINES OF METALLIC GOLD 10/0
❘	AB FINISHED EMERALD GREEN #2 BUGLE BEAD

❙	METALLIC GOLD #2 BUGLE BEAD
Ⓟ	3-MM FRESHWATER PEARL
▲	DRAPE NUMBER OF AMBER AB 11/0 SEED BEADS ON DOUBLE THREAD BETWEEN ▲
●	FILL BACKGROUND WITH GOLD 12/0 THREE CUT BEADS
----	LINES OF GOLD 12/0 THREE CUT

*R*ainbow Trimmed Shirt

One purchased shirt with pointed collar
11/0 seed beads:
    600 lustered salmon
    600 lustered rose
    600 lustered lavender
    600 lustered medium blue
    600 lustered aqua

Thread
Dressmaker's pen

DIRECTIONS

Measure and mark ⅜" to ½" intervals around collar.
Using thread doubled, stitch beaded rows, beginning
with salmon. Continue as follows: rose, lavender, blue,
and aqua; see diagram.

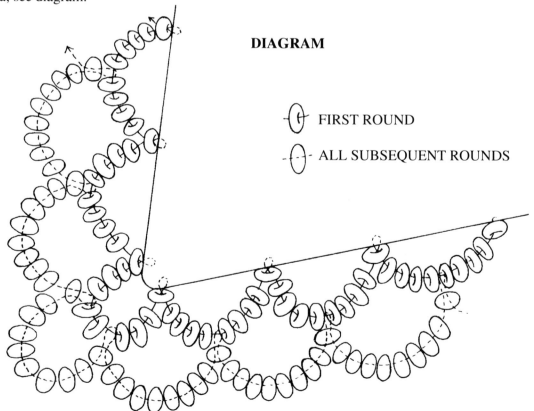

DIAGRAM

FIRST ROUND

ALL SUBSEQUENT ROUNDS

Narrow Scarf

MATERIALS

¼ yard of fabric
666 AB finished transparent blue 12/0 two-cut beads
36 orchid 11/0 seed beads

72 transparent amethyst 8/0 seed beads
36 lustered red 6/0 seed beads
36 aqua #2 bugle beads

DIRECTIONS

All seams are ⅜".

1. From fabric, cut two 3" x 60" strips. Cut short ends at a diagonal; see Diagram A.

2. With right sides facing and edges aligned, stitch strips together, leaving a small opening in side. Clip corners at each end; see Diagram B. Turn; whipstitch closed. Press flat.

3. To make fringe, begin at short side of diagonal cut. Thread ten 12/0 two-cut beads, one 8/0, one #2 bugle, one 8/0, one 6/0, and one 11/0 seed bead. Refer to General Instructions for "Fringes" on page 139. Repeat, increasing until ending with 27 12/0 two-cut beads; see Diagram C. Repeat on other end of scarf.

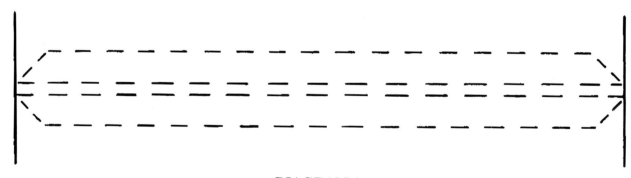

DIAGRAM A

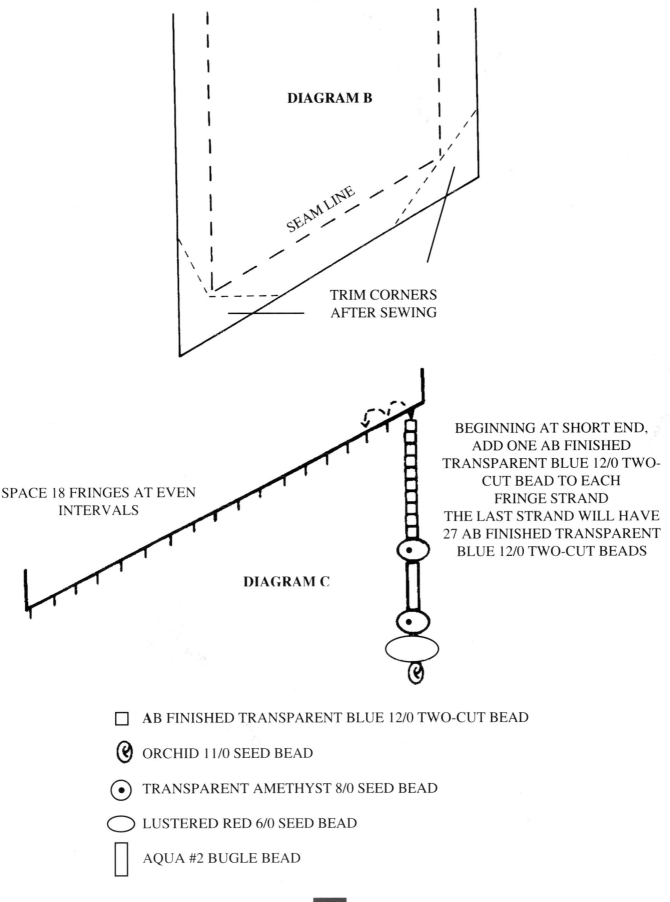

DIAGRAM B

SEAM LINE

TRIM CORNERS
AFTER SEWING

SPACE 18 FRINGES AT EVEN
INTERVALS

BEGINNING AT SHORT END,
ADD ONE AB FINISHED
TRANSPARENT BLUE 12/0 TWO-
CUT BEAD TO EACH
FRINGE STRAND
THE LAST STRAND WILL HAVE
27 AB FINISHED TRANSPARENT
BLUE 12/0 TWO-CUT BEADS

DIAGRAM C

☐ **AB FINISHED TRANSPARENT BLUE 12/0 TWO-CUT BEAD**

Ⓠ ORCHID 11/0 SEED BEAD

⊙ TRANSPARENT AMETHYST 8/0 SEED BEAD

◯ LUSTERED RED 6/0 SEED BEAD

▯ AQUA #2 BUGLE BEAD

Cherub Necklace

11/0 seed beads:
    approximately 800 bronze
    approximately 800 silver
    approximately 225 gold
5 yards of size 0 nylon thread

One clasp set
Two end caps
One jump ring
Porcelain cherub or charm of choice
Glue

DIRECTIONS

1. Cut seven 24" lengths of nylon.

2. Thread seed beads on each length as follows: 15 bronze, 1 gold, 2 bronze, 1 gold, 1 bronze, 2 gold, 1 bronze, 6 gold, 1 silver, 3 gold, 1 silver, 2 gold, 3 silver, 1 gold, 4⅛" of silver, 1 gold, 3 silver, 1 gold, 1 silver, 2 gold, 1 silver, 3 gold, 1 silver, 6 gold, 1 bronze, 2 gold, 1 bronze, 1 gold, 2 bronze, 1 gold, 3¾" of bronze. Reverse pattern, ending with 15 bronze. Each strand will be about 20".

3. Tie all seven ends together on each side, making sure there is little slack. Make a second knot over the first at both ends. Glue; let dry.

4. Cut all but the longest loose ends of nylon. Thread end on needle, sew through cap and one side of clasp, back through glued knot. Repeat until secured. Knot will disappear into cap.

5. Handling seven strands as one, loosely tie a knot in center of bronze section. Open and loop jump ring around two or three bead strands in middle of center knot. Slip the ring through the cherub's loop and close the jump ring.

END CAP

CLIP ALL BUT
ONE THREAD

REMAINING THREAD GOES THROUGH CAP
AND ONE SIDE OF CLASP, THEN BACK
THROUGH GLUED KNOT. (REPEAT A FEW
TIMES UNTIL SECURE.) CLIP THREAD CLOSE.
KNOT SHOULD DISAPPEAR INTO CAP

DIAGRAM

Cherub Tapestry Vest

MATERIALS

One large-size vest
3,250 11/0 seed beads in color of choice
   (Note: 45 beads equals 1" of trim)

Thread to match
Pins

DIRECTIONS

1. Using pins, mark edge of vest in ¼" intervals; see Diagram A. Start at shoulder and secure doubled thread to vest.

2. Work row 1; see Diagram B. Remove pins after attaching loop. Work row 2 into row 1; see Diagram B.

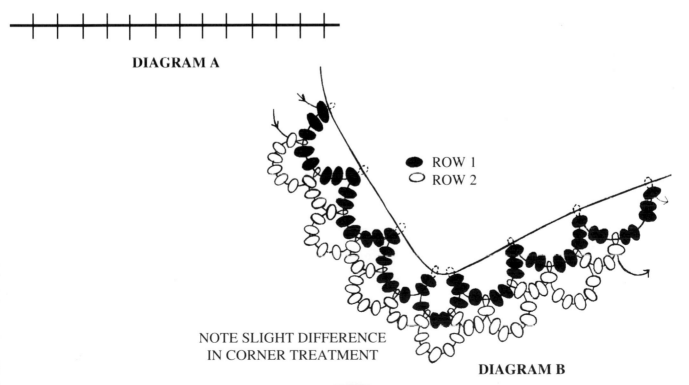

DIAGRAM A

ROW 1
ROW 2

NOTE SLIGHT DIFFERENCE
IN CORNER TREATMENT

DIAGRAM B

Bronze Fringe Scarf

MATERIALS

Purchased scarf in which width is a multiple of 1¾"
196 bronze 11/0 seed beads

Three iris purple 5-mm teardrop crystals
One bronze 8-mm crystal

DIRECTIONS

Work each 1¾" section separately. "X" marks the beginning of each section. "◆" shows where to end the last section; see diagram on page 108.

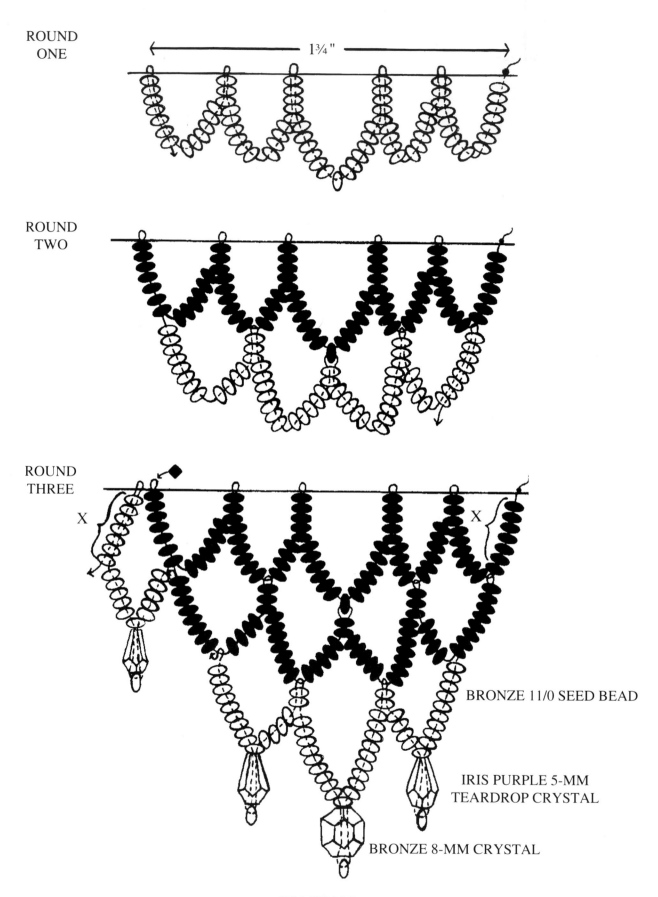

ROUND
ONE

1¾"

ROUND
TWO

ROUND
THREE

X   X

BRONZE 11/0 SEED BEAD

IRIS PURPLE 5-MM
TEARDROP CRYSTAL

BRONZE 8-MM CRYSTAL

DIAGRAM

$\mathcal{D}$ual Colored Scarf

MATERIALS

¼ yard of fabric
¼ yard of contrasting fabric for backing
1750 iris blue 12/0 three-cut beads

1610 bronze 11/0 seed beads
70 bronze 6/0 seed beads
70 AB finished emerald #2 bugle beads
70 cobalt 4-mm x 6-mm glass beads

DIRECTIONS

All seams are ⅜".

1. From fabric, cut one 6" x 43" strip. From contrasting fabric, cut one 6" x 43" strip. Cut short ends of each strip at a diagonal; see Diagram A.

2. With right sides facing and edges aligned, stitch strips together, leaving a small opening in side; see Diagram A. Clip corners; see Diagram B. Turn; whipstitch closed. Press flat.

3. Stitch 35 bead fringes to scarf at even intervals; see Diagram C. Refer to General Instructions for "Fringes" on page 139.

☐ IRIS BLUE 12/0 THREE-CUT BEAD

◯ BRONZE 11/0 SEED BEAD

⬭ BRONZE 6/0 SEED BEAD

▭ AB FINISHED EMERALD #2 BUGLE BEAD

⬭ COBALT 4-MM X 6-MM GLASS BEAD

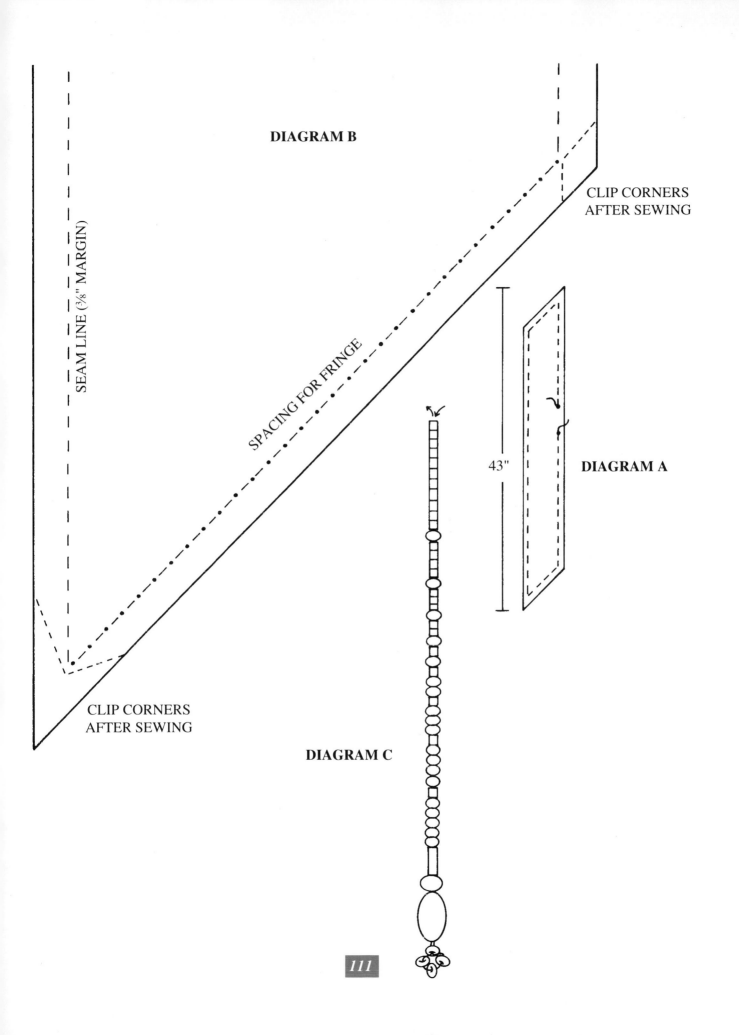

DIAGRAM B

SEAM LINE (⅜" MARGIN)

CLIP CORNERS
AFTER SEWING

SPACING FOR FRINGE

CLIP CORNERS
AFTER SEWING

43"

DIAGRAM A

DIAGRAM C

Southwest Earrings

MATERIALS

One pair of earwires
Two nine-holed dome discs
Two .21 gauge headpins
Two turquoise 10-mm beads
Four lavender 4-mm ceramic beads
Ten lavender 6-mm ceramic beads
Four opaque aqua 11/0 seed beads
60 opaque amethyst 11/0 seed beads

18 opaque aqua 8/0 seed beads
Six iris blue matte 6/0 seed beads
18 copper 6/0 seed beads
Ten iris blue matte #2 bugle beads
Four aqua matte 15-mm ceramic tubes
18 graduated flat-end pins
Wire cutters
Needle-nose pliers

DIRECTIONS

1. Thread beads onto headpins; see diagram.

2. Trim headpins with wire cutters so that ½" of unbeaded pin remains above top bead.

3. Using needle-nose pliers, bend tops of headpins and slip each headpin through the appropriate hole in the nine-hole disks. Close each loop to secure the hanger to the disk. Attach the disks to the earwires; see diagram.

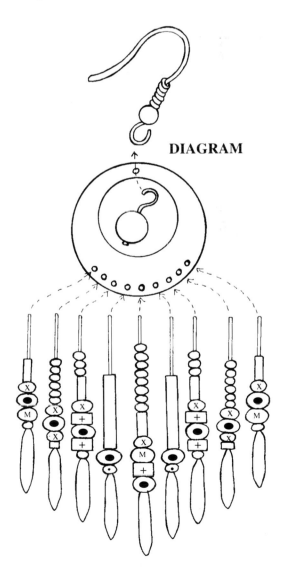

DIAGRAM

☐ LAVENDER 4-MM CERAMIC BEAD

⬭ OPAQUE AMETHYST 11/0 SEED BEAD

⊙ OPAQUE AQUA 11/0 SEED BEAD

Ⓧ OPAQUE AQUA 8/0 SEED BEAD

Ⓜ IRIS BLUE MATTE 6/0 SEED BEAD

⬤ COPPER 6/0 SEED BEAD

+ LAVENDER 6-MM CERAMIC BEAD

▯ IRIS BLUE MATTE #2 BUGLE BEAD

▯ AQUA MATTE 15-MM CERAMIC TUBE

113

Chevron Scarf

MATERIALS

⅜ yard of lightweight silk
70 turquoise matte #2 bugle beads
1428 iris purple 12/0 three-cut beads

348 metallic gold 12/0 three-cut beads
54 iris topaz matte 6/0 beads

DIRECTIONS

All seams are ½".

1. From lightweight silk, cut two 5" x 37" pieces. Cut short ends at a point; see Diagram A.

2. With right sides facing and edges aligned, stitch strips together, leaving a small opening in side; see Diagram A. Clip corners; see Diagram B. Turn; whipstitch closed. Press flat.

3. Stitch 27 fringes in even intervals to end of scarf; see Diagram C. Refer to General Instructions for "Fringes" on page 139. Repeat on other end of scarf.

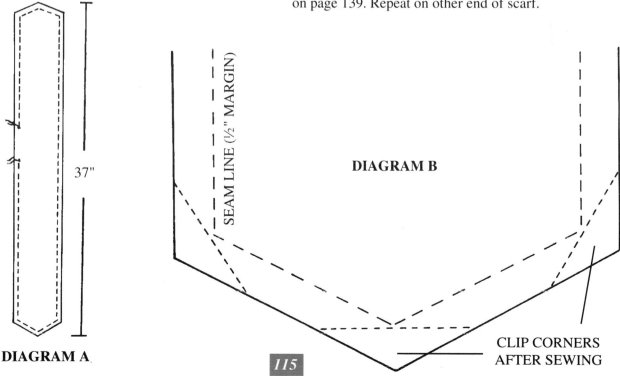

37"

DIAGRAM A

SEAM LINE (½" MARGIN)

DIAGRAM B

CLIP CORNERS
AFTER SEWING

TURQUOISE MATTE #2 BUGLE BEAD

IRIS PURPLE 12/0 THREE-CUT BEAD

METALLIC GOLD 12/0 THREE-CUT BEAD

IRIS TOPAZ MATTE 6/0 BEAD

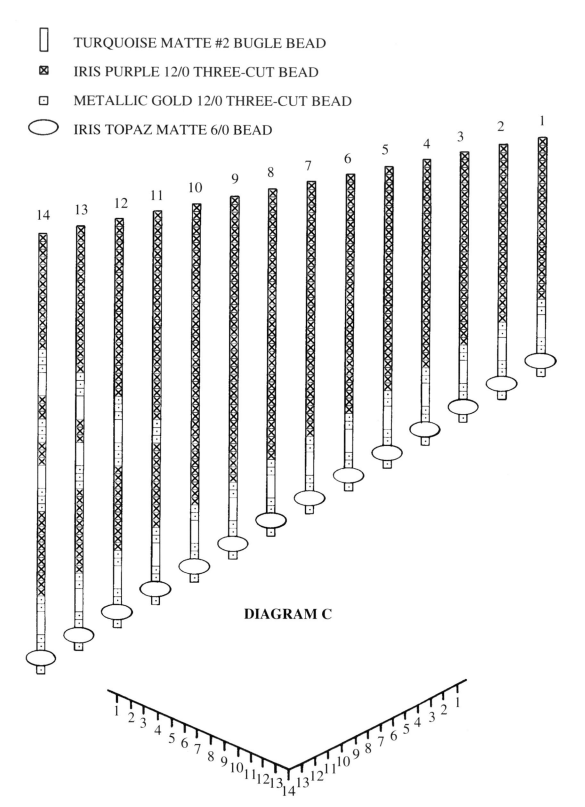

DIAGRAM C

Cowboy Boot Clips

MATERIALS

One pair of toe ornament findings
Two 1¼" silver conchos with one hole at bottom
Two 1"-diameter nine-hole silver disks; see diagram
Twenty .021 gauge 2½" headpins
Six 10-mm matte amethyst disks, center holes
Twelve 6-mm lavender ceramic cylinders
½ oz. of metallic copper 11/0 seed beads
26 light metallic copper 6/0 seed beads
30 opaque aqua 8/0 seed beads

24 opaque amethyst 8/0 seed beads
20 matte coral 6/0 seed beads
Two 10-mm turquoise disks
16 iris turquoise matte #2 bugle beads
Double-sided adhesive pads
Wire cutters
Needle-nose pliers

DIRECTIONS

1. Thread beads onto headpins; see diagram. Make two of A and four each of B, C, D, and E.

2. Trim headpins with wire cutters so that ⅜" of unbeaded pin remains above top bead.

3. Using needle-nose pliers, bend tops of headpins and slip each headpin through the appropriate hole in the nine-hole disk. Close each loop to secure the hanger to the disk.

4. Attach the disk to the concho; see diagram.

5. Attach toe findings to back of concho using double-sided adhesive pads. If the back surface of the concho is curved, use a double layer of adhesive pad to secure the finding.

6. Attach clips to the top center of your cowboy boots.

DIAGRAM

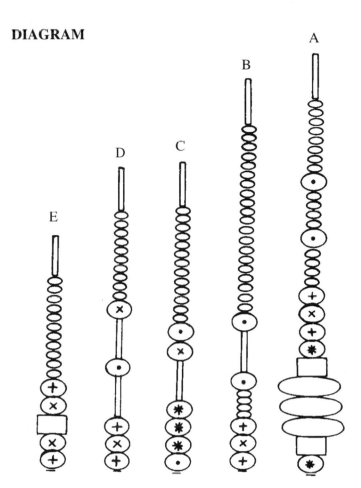

○ METALLIC COPPER 11/0 SEED BEAD

⊙ OPAQUE AMETHYST 8/0 SEED BEAD

⊕ OPAQUE AQUA 8/0 SEED BEAD

⊛ MATTE CORAL 6/0 SEED BEAD

⊗ LIGHT METALLIC COPPER 6/0 SEED BEAD

▯ IRIS TURQUOISE MATTE #2 BUGLE BEAD

▭ LAVENDER CERAMIC CYLINDER

⬭ 10-MM MATTE AMETHYST DISK

⬬ 10-MM TURQUOISE DISK

Leopard Skin Hat Band

MATERIALS

One purchased hat
11/0 seed beads for each pattern repeat:
   34 black
   73 copper
   414 cream
   127 AB finished dark topaz
   251 AB finished light topaz

1 yard of ¾" cotton cording
Thread

DIRECTIONS

1. Measure around hat, weave pattern on page 122, repeating as needed for measured length; refer to General Instructions for "Needleweaving" on page 133.

2. Stitch long edges of beaded strip around cotton cording; refer to General Instructions for "Finishing a Tube" on page 140.

3. Cut cording to same length as beaded strip. Push back beaded ends; stitch cording ends together. Stitch beaded ends together. Slide onto hat.

⬭   11/0 CREAM SEED BEAD

⬓   11/0 AB FINISHED LIGHT TOPAZ SEED BEAD

⊠   11/0 AB FINISHED DARK TOPAZ SEED BEAD

⬥   11/0 COPPER SEED BEAD

⬤   11/0 BLACK SEED BEAD

LEOPARD SKIN HAT BAND PATTERN

General Instructions

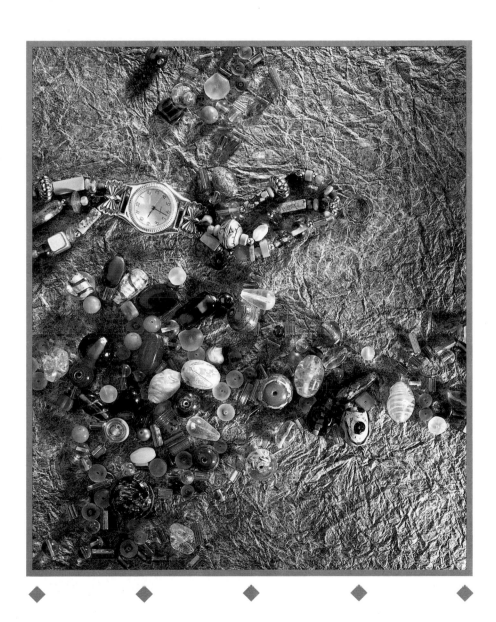

◆   ◆   ◆   ◆   ◆

General Instructions

About Beads

Although most beads are machine manufactured, it is essentially a hand-making process. There is a tremendous amount of variation from one bead to the next in each of the standard bead sizes. These odd-shaped beads can be beneficial and charming when used in some designs. However, to avoid frustration, when the hole in a bead is so tight it does not slip easily over the needle, discard the bead.

Removing Unwanted Beads

If you wish to remove beads from a section that is puckering or if you have accidentally sewn on the wrong bead, break them off with medium-sized, all-purpose pliers. Use caution when breaking off beads, as fragments can get in your eyes.

Thread Hints

Soaping or waxing the thread keeps it from tangling. Run the thread across the surface of the soap or wax; then pull the thread between your fingertips to remove any excess.

Bead-Handling Tips

Who spilled the beads? There's no use crying over spilled beads. Instead, try putting a new bag in your vacuum cleaner. Wet the tip of your finger to pick up just a few beads.

They're all wet! A moistened paper towel, wrung out a little, reduces the static electricity that builds up around glass beads. Place the wet towel on your flat container while working.

Mexican jumping beads! If you store your beads in a plastic bag, they will probably try to jump out when you open it up. Blow into the bag lightly and the moisture from your breath will settle the beads enough to pour them out.

Temptation. It is very tempting to loop away without recounting your beads after threading on a very long row. You will only do this once. If you have to rip out a row, first, pull the needle off the thread. Then, use the tip of the needle to gently pull the thread out of the beads.

Organization. Sort beads and place them in small containers with flat, small lipped lids. A muffin tin may also come in handy as a useful organizer.

Surfaces, Needles, and Thread

The designs in this book call for many different surfaces. Some designs are stitched on felt, others on card stock (any form of lightweight cardboard such as heavyweight construction paper or a manila folder, depending on the stiffness you desire); some are worked on leather. The only difference, when beading on different surfaces, is the needle and thread you choose. Leather requires a very sharp, strong needle—ordinary beading needles are not a good choice. Try using a #10 quilting needle and ordinary sewing thread. When beading on very soft, fine fabrics, a regular beading needle is an appropriate choice and you can use fine silk thread. Felt requires no special needle or thread for successful stitching. If you are beading on card stock, a #9 embroidery needle or a #10 quilting needle will work well and ordinary sewing thread is a good choice.

Patterns

The method used to transfer the design onto the beading surface will also vary with the type of surface you choose. If you are not covering the surface entirely, it will be important for your design lines to be invisible afterward.

On very lightweight fabrics, you can simply place the fabric over the design and trace it, especially if you work on a transparent surface with light coming up from underneath, such as a glass tabletop or light table. Ordinary graphite pencil marks, when made with a light touch, will wash out later with mild detergent. Always test the fabric before washing.

Felt can be handled more roughly. Always pre-shrink felt with a hot steam iron before transferring the design onto it. A great way to deal with felt is to make a heat transfer using special transfer pens or pencils available in some art or needlework stores. Trace the design on tracing paper; then turn it face down and retrace it in the transfer pencil. Iron the design onto the felt with a hot iron, holding the iron in each position for about 12 to 15 seconds. This method also works well for any fabric that has a high synthetic content, such as polyester or acrylic. Always pre-shrink, or the transfer lines will be smudged. Remember that lines made with transfer ink or pencil will not ever wash out under any circumstances. They become part of the fabric.

The best method for transferring the design onto card stock is simply to photocopy the page directly. Since the authors and publishers of this book grant their permission to photocopy patterns, there is no violation of copyright law in doing so.

If a photocopier is unavailable to you, try the following method. You will need tracing paper, carbon paper and a writing utensil with a sharp point. Lay the tracing paper over the pattern and trace all information. Lay carbon paper, carbon side down, on the surface of the bead card. Lay the traced pattern on carbon paper. Retrace all pattern information to the bead card.

Slipstitch

Slipstitch is an almost invisible stitch used to join edges. Using a single strand of thread knotted at one end, insert the needle at 1 and bring it out at 2, picking up a few threads. Slide the needle under the folded edge of the fabric ¼", bringing it out at 3 on the edge; see Diagram A.

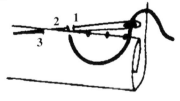

DIAGRAM A

Couching

Couching is a sewing technique used to anchor objects to any surface. With thread, bring the needle up at 1, down at 2. Repeat to attach the entire length as desired; see Diagram B.

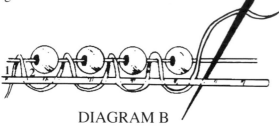

DIAGRAM B

Fusing

To fuse backing fabric to beaded projects, you will need a thick white towel, stitched bead card, fusible webbing with paper removed, fabric, a sheet of clean white paper and an iron.

Layer and center the components; see Diagram C. Press the iron down flat for five seconds. Shift the iron and press for two seconds more to eliminate any steam holes. Allow the piece to cool completely. With nail scissors, trim excess card and fabric. Run a thin line of diluted white glue around the entire outside edge to secure.

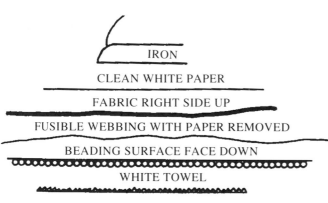

DIAGRAM C

Sewing Seed Beads

For small areas and tight curves, it is best to sew on each bead individually. Bring the needle up from back to front through the beading surface in the desired location. Slip the bead over the needle and guide it all the way down the thread until it rests on the beading surface in the desired place. Bring the needle back through the beading surface right in the same hole or very close by so that the bead is secured to the surface; see Diagram D.

TWO HOLES

SAME HOLE

DIAGRAM D

For gentle curves and outlines, seed beads may be sewn on two at a time; see Diagram E. Poke a hole through the beading surface about two bead lengths forward on the stitching line (hole A). Bring the needle up from back to front. Slip two beads on the needle, letting them slide all the way down the thread until they are on their round sides on the stitching line. Bring the needle down through the beading surface from front to back (hole B) so that the two beads are secured. Poke another hole in the stitching line about two bead lengths forward (hole C). Bring the needle up from back to front and slip on two more beads. Slide them to the surface and bring the needle from front to back in the first hole made (hole A). Repeat these steps for the length of the line.

DIAGRAM E

Backtracking

After completing a line of seed beads, fortify the line with backtracking. Bring the needle up just past the last bead in the line, and run the thread back through all the beads in the line. Just after the last bead, bring the needle to the back of the beading surface and secure the thread. This is especially important for outlines around the outside edge of a design. If the beads being backtracked have very fine holes, it may be necessary to use a #10 needle. It will help to run through only three beads at a time, particularly if the line is curved. Keep running through until all the beads in one line are joined together by a single thread; see Diagram F. Tighten it until the line is smooth and neat (but not so tight that there is puckering).

BACKTRACKING THREAD

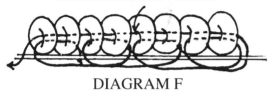

DIAGRAM F

For filling large areas, you may sew several beads at one time, provided they are anchored with small stitches along the length of the line (similar to the needlecraft technique known as couching). Bring the needle up at your chosen starting place and slip on several beads, laying them against the beading surface to see if they fill the desired space comfortably; see Diagram G. Small gaps in the beads will not be noticeable, but large gaps and puckering will be unattractive in the finished work. Try to space the beads so that they touch each other gently, but are not crowded. Cramming six beads into a five-bead length will be far more noticeable than the tiny gaps that naturally occur between the rounded edges of beads sewn close to each other.

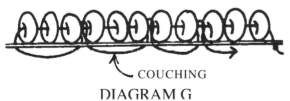

COUCHING
DIAGRAM G

Note: The techniques just described are used when sewing seed beads in sizes 8/0 through 16/0. Larger seed beads, especially E-beads (size 6/0) and pony beads (sizes 5/0 and 4/0), are sewn on individually because of their weight and larger size. Outlines of E-beads and pony beads should be backtracked with thread of a closely coordinated color because the thread can show in the relatively larger gap between beads.

Sewing Bugle Beads

Bugle beads are almost always sewn on individually. Bring the needle from back to front through the beading surface. Then, slip on the bugle bead, allowing it to rest against the surface. At the other end of the bead, bring the needle back through the beading surface, pulling the thread until the bead rests firmly against the beading surface; see Diagram H.

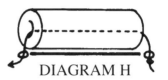

DIAGRAM H

A long line of bugle beads placed end-to-end may be sewn on at one time, provided you anchor the line to the beading surface in several places; see Diagram I. You may want to backtrack the line to firm it up and stabilize it. Since some bugle beads have extremely fine holes, you will probably need to use a #10 quilting needle to backtrack bugle beads. You may have to run through each bead individually when backtracking.

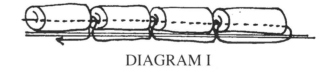

DIAGRAM I

Large bugle beads (#5 and longer) may be sewn on individually as just described. One concern in sewing on any bugle bead, but especially larger ones, is the possibility that the cut end of the glass tube will cut or fray your thread. This is one reason why the thread is never tightened to the point of puckering. When bugle beads are sewn in a fan-shaped area, there will be small gaps between them in some places; see Diagram J. Ignore these spaces, as they will not be particularly noticeable in your finished piece. If they are truly bothersome to you, lightly paint on a thin wash of pale gray watercolor using a small brush. This will soften the appearance of the surface between the beads.

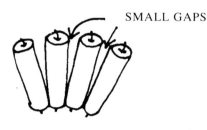

SMALL GAPS

DIAGRAM J

Sewing Crystals

Crystals are sewn on so that one of the cut facets lies flat against the beading surface. Place the unsewn crystal on the surface in its desired position, and poke a hole at one end. Bring the needle up from back to front through this hole, and slip the crystal on, allowing it to rest against the surface in its final position. Bring the needle from front to back at the other end of the crystal; see Diagram K.

DIAGRAM K

Very small crystals (4-mm or 5-mm) can essentially be treated much as seed beads are treated. They can be sewn on in lines and backtracked or sewn on individually, depending on the final position. Larger crystals (6-mm to 12-mm) require some additional treatment such as a cross-stitch. Stitch up from the lower left; then slip on crystal and bring needle down through the card at the upper right. Secure crystal by returning thread through crystal, lower right to upper left; see Diagram L.

TOP VIEW

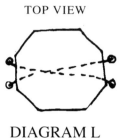

DIAGRAM L

Since there will be some thread visible at each end of the crystal, you may choose to slip on one or two small seed beads prior to slipping on the crystal. Then use one or two small seed beads at the other end of the thread as well; see Diagram M.

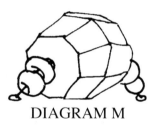

DIAGRAM M

Sewing Freshwater Pearls

Pearls have extremely fine holes, and you will have to use a #10 quilting needle. Bring the needle up from back to front through the beading surface; then slip the pearl on, allowing it to rest on the surface; see Diagram N. Note that most freshwater pearls have one side that is slightly flattened. This side should be touching the beading surface and the attractive, rounded side should face up. It is nearly impossible to backtrack all freshwater pearls. If they are used in a continuous line, sew them on carefully to insure an attractive appearance.

DIAGRAM N

Sewing Semiprecious Chips

Most semiprecious chips are drilled through the short side. Position the chip as desired unsewn on the beading surface. Bring the needle from back to front through the beading surface and slip the chip over the needle until the chip rests flat against the surface. Slide one small seed bead over the needle; then insert the needle back through the chip hole. Pull the thread tight until the small seed bead acts as an anchor on the top surface of the chip; see Diagram O.

DIAGRAM O

Sewing Odd-Shaped Beads

In general, the shape of the bead determines which method of sewing will be best. If a bead is donut-shaped, it will probably be best sewn using the technique used for semiprecious chips. Long narrow beads may be treated in a similar manner to bugle beads. Faceted or large round beads can be sewn on much like faceted crystals. Below are examples of how to deal with odd beads; see Diagram P.

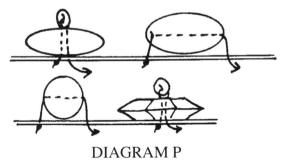

DIAGRAM P

Sewing on Lace

Almost any lace can be embellished with beads. Most fabric stores carry a tremendous variety of lace patterns, so if you engage in a little creative thinking, you can surely find great materials. Follow these simple guidelines to dress up the lace of your choice:

♦ Choose lace that is substantial enough to carry the weight of the beads you are using, or choose beads that are light enough to suit your lace.

♦ Use ordinary sewing thread to sew beads onto lace; best results will be achieved if you match the color of the thread to the color of the lace.

♦ Try to keep your stitches hidden. In the example given below, the path of the thread is shown; it is entirely buried within the lace itself.

♦ Choose beads that are suitable to the theme of your lace. If, for example, the pattern you choose has a floral theme, try using rounded beads as the centers of rounded flowers and bugle beads to accent spiky leaves.

- 11/0 seed beads

6-mm crystal

#3 bugle bead

3-mm freshwater pearl

Thread knot

Path of thread

Sewing on Needlepoint Canvas

Beads are sewn individually to the intersection of the two canvas threads, just as in regular needlepoint, in which one stitch is formed over the intersection of two canvas threads. The appearance of the finished work is quite similar to needlepoint, because each oblong oval bead is approximately the same size and shape as a traditional half-cross-stitch.

Experienced needlepointers will be hesitant initially to run the thread in a different direction. In order to make the bead slant to the right, the thread must slant to the left. Additionally, a beading or fine embroidery needle must be used, which will feel very tiny to a stitcher accustomed to the firm bulk of a tapestry needle.

Here are some rules for beading on needlepoint canvas:

♦ Use interlock (single thread lock-weave) canvas or double threaded (Penelope) canvas. Mono (single thread overweave) canvas is too unstable for use with beads.

♦ Use a #9 embroidery needle or a #10 quilting needle. They are shorter than most beading needles and will be easier to handle.

♦ Use doubled ordinary sewing thread matched to the color of the canvas. If you are beading on a painted canvas and do not wish to keep an assortment of threads around to match your colors, use a neutral medium gray.

♦ It is far easier to count one horizontal row at a time than to wander all around the canvas as you work. Mark off each row after completion; it will help you keep track of your place.

♦ Use 11/0 seed beads on 14-count canvas; use 14/0 seed beads on 18-count canvas.

♦ If possible, paint the design on the canvas before beading, following your stitching chart.

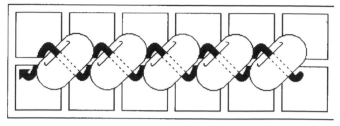

SHORT BACKSTITCH

DOES NOT DISTORT CANVAS

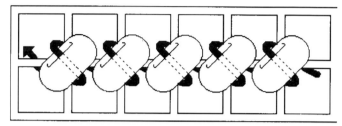

LONG BACKSTITCH

DISTORTS CANVAS VERY SLIGHTLY. CAN BE COR-RECTED BY PRESSING BACK OF FINISHED WORK WITH STEAM IRON. THEN, PULL FABRIC UNTIL ORIGINAL SHAPE IS RESTORED. (USE CAUTION! BEADS WILL RETAIN THE HEAT OF THE IRON)

Finishing Needlepoint Canvas

1. Trim excess to ½". Notch corners and outside curves; clip inside curves; see Diagram Q.

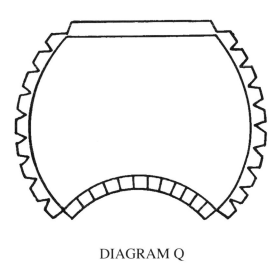

DIAGRAM Q

2. Press trimmed edges down flat against back or work; see Diagram R.

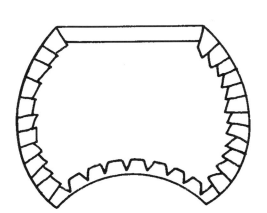

DIAGRAM R

3. Use trimmed, pressed piece as template to cut lining, adding ½" to all edges; see Diagram S. Trim and press lining as in Step 1.

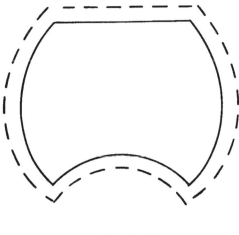

DIAGRAM S

4. Use matching thread and tiny stitches to slipstitch lining to back of canvas; see Diagram T.

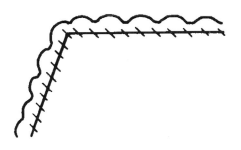

DIAGRAM T

Backings for Odd-Shaped Pieces

1. Use finished design piece to cut lining, backing, and interfacing, adding ½" to all edges; see Diagram U. (Use felt if more stiffness is desired.)

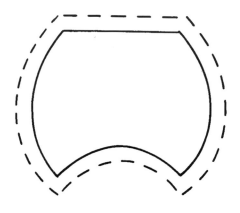

DIAGRAM U

2. Layer lining right side up, backing right side down, and interfacing. Baste with loose stitches; see Diagram V.

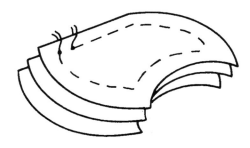

DIAGRAM V

3. Sew all edges, leaving an opening for turning; see Diagram W.

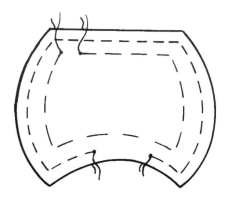

DIAGRAM W

4. Trim interfacing to the seam line. Notch corners and curves of lining and backing. Turn right side out. Press edges flat. Slipstitch opening; see Diagram X.

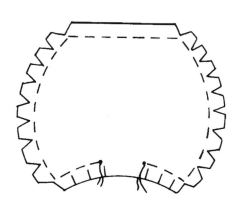

DIAGRAM X

Getting Started

Basic needleweaving may remind you of crocheting. The first row is worked; then subsequent rows are looped into the first row in a predictable way. Unlike crochet, which is usually worked from written directions, bead needleweaving is worked from a gridded pattern (except when weaving a sphere, which is worked from written directions).

Vertical rows of counted beads are attached to the previous vertical rows by a series of evenly spaced loops. The ideal pattern is to loop after every third bead. In some cases, where great strength is needed, you may want to loop more frequently.

The first few rows are somewhat unstable and may seem difficult to work. Tricks for dealing with this temporary instability are described on the following pages. Be patient! After two or three rows, the weaving will be quite easy to handle.

Gather together your materials and tools, follow the step-by-step instructions, and enjoy!

Needles

Because of their great length, traditional beading needles are not well suited for needleweaving. A #9 embroidery needle is ideal when working with seed beads size 11 or larger. For some finely drilled stones and pearls, a #10 quilting needle is recommended.

Thread Types

Ordinary mercerized cotton sewing thread is recommended for most needleweaving. Choose a neutral color that is similar in theme to your bead design. It is nearly impossible to weave without a little thread showing between the beads, so try to minimize the distraction by using compatible thread.

Light nylon may be used, but it has greater bulk than ordinary sewing thread and should be restricted to uses where strength is a consideration. If you are using a lot of valuable stones or your beadweaving piece is supporting any weight, nylon may be a necessary choice.

Fine silk or cotton embroidery floss are good choices for use in needleweaving. Separate the plies of cotton 6-ply embroidery floss and use only one ply at a time.

Metallic threads are not recommended because the surface fiber tends to fray and ravel. When pulling metallic thread through a tight-fitting bead, fibers will bunch up around the bead opening.

Adding a New Thread

When about 3" of thread remains unbeaded on the needle, it is time to add a new thread. Remove the needle from the old thread; see Diagram Y. Cut a new 30" length. A longer piece will tend to tangle, and a shorter piece will require frequent additions of thread.

Tie a square knot so that the knot lands about 1" from where the old thread emerges from the beadwork; see Diagram Z. Place a tiny dot of glue on the knot. Wipe off any excess glue, but you don't need to wait for the glue to dry before proceeding.

Continue beading as if you were using one continuous thread. Let the thread ends protrude from the work until the new thread is well established within the weave; see Diagram A. Then, pull gently on the ends and clip them close so that they disappear into the weave. You may find it necessary to use a smaller needle until you have passed the area of the knot.

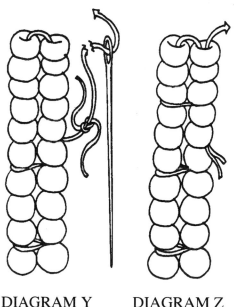

DIAGRAM Y   DIAGRAM Z

Seed Bead Needleweaving

The following instructions illustrate the basic technique of bead needleweaving. Acquaint yourself with this technique by experimenting with the instructions and diagrams on the next few pages. Before you know it, you will have discovered the magic of "beauty and the beads."

In these instructions, the vertical rows are numbered from left to right. Row 1 is leftmost for a right-handed person. A left-handed person should start with the highest numbered row and work right to left. The work always proceeds the direction of your dominant hand. The beads of each row are numbered from 1, beginning at the top of each vertical row and increasing to the bottom of the row. The diagrams show a 12-bead row.

Cut a length of thread about 30" long and thread the needle so that a 5" tail remains. A longer thread will tend to tangle, and a shorter thread will necessitate frequent rethreadings.

Slip one bead of any color over the needle, and position it about 3" from the long end of the thread. Loop the thread back through the bead and pull it tightly. The purpose of this "stopper" bead is to keep the design pattern beads from slipping off the needle. It will be removed after a few rows. Secure the stopper bead to a flat or slightly curved surface to stabilize the thread. Some suggestions are a tabletop, the arm of a chair, or a small cushion.

Thread the beads of row 1 from top to bottom; see Diagram AA. Skip the last bead threaded, inserting the needle back through all the beads on the thread. The needle should emerge from the top bead of row 1.

Draw a line through the first vertical row of the chart to show that it has been completed.

Thread the beads of row 2, again reading from top to bottom; see Diagram BB. Always recount the beads against the pattern to be sure they are in order.

ROW 1

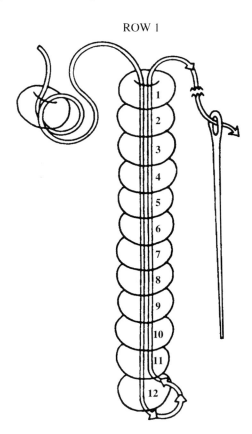

DIAGRAM AA

ROW 1   ROW 2

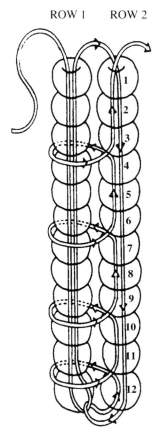

DIAGRAM BB

Insert the needle into the loop exposed at the bottom of row 1. Pull the thread gently until the whole second row is taut but not tight and can rest against the first row without much puckering.

Insert the needle into the last bead of row 2 (bead 12) and bring the thread out until it is taut but not tight. Loop the thread around row 1 so that it nestles in the space between beads 12 and 11 of row 2, bringing the needle out in the space between beads 10 and 9 on row 2. Again, bring the thread taut but not tight.

Loop the thread around row 1 so that the thread nestles in the space between beads 10 and 9 of row 1. Insert the needle into the next three beads on row 2 (beads 9, 8 and 7) and bring the needle out in the space between beads 7 and 6 on row 2.

Tighten the thread again, then loop it around the first row so that it nestles in the space between beads 7 and 6 on row 1. Insert the needle into the next three beads on row 2 (beads 6, 5 and 4) and repeat the looping-inserting process until the thread emerges from bead 1 of row 2. After row 2, you may no longer need to stabilize the work. It will get easier and easier to handle as the weaving grows.

All subsequent rows will be worked the same, except that the first loop (nestled between beads 12 and 11 on row 1) will not be made. It is added to the first row to stabilize the work, but is not especially needed in the following rows. The pattern of loops may be worked in any way. If you wish to make a loop between every bead, you may do so, but a three-bead repeat is the most effective for needleweaving. The more frequently you loop, the stiffer the woven piece will be.

ROW 1   ROW 2   ROW 3

AND BEYOND

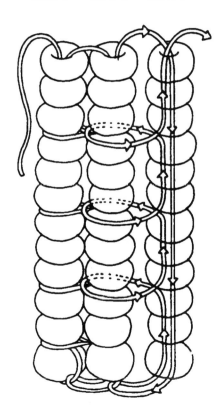

DIAGRAM CC

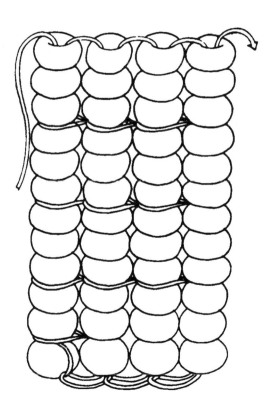

DIAGRAM DD

Bugle Bead Needleweaving

Bugle beads are longer than seed beads and therefore the weave goes quickly. This makes bugle beads well suited to any project that might otherwise be tedious and time consuming. Try using them for purses, belts, bracelets or straps.

Weaving with bugle beads is essentially the same process as weaving with seed beads. The major difference is that in weaving with bugle beads, you should loop between every bead. In weaving with seed beads, you can skip beads and still have a very stable and attractive result. Skipping a loop while weaving bugle beads can mean gaps in the weave and puckering of the finished piece.

It is very important to pay special attention to the tension of your thread while weaving. This is especially important on the first row in which the tone for the entire piece will be established.

Because the holes in bugle beads can be quite small, it is probably a good idea to start with a tiny needle.

Inspect the bugles to see if any are broken or obviously different in length. Try to use beads which are similar in length, or there will be some puckering.

Place a stopper bead on the end of your 30" thread. Thread all beads of the first vertical row. Skip the last bead and run the needle back through all the remaining beads on the thread; see Diagram EE. Be especially careful to keep the tension of the thread loose so that the bottom bead does not twist.

Thread all beads of row 2. Insert the needle into the bottom bead on row 1 and pull the thread all the way through. Then, insert the needle into the second-to-bottom bead of row 2 and pull the thread all the way through. Loop around row 1 so that the loop nestles in the space between beads. Insert the needle in the next bugle bead on row 2 and repeat the looping process until the needle emerges from the top bugle of row 2; see Diagram FF.

Thread all bugles of row 3. Run the needle through the small piece of thread that connects the bottom bugles of rows 1 and 2. Insert the needle back into the bottom bead of row 3. Continue looping as in the previous rows until the thread emerges from the top of row 3; see Diagram GG. All subsequent rows will be connected at the bottom bead in this manner.

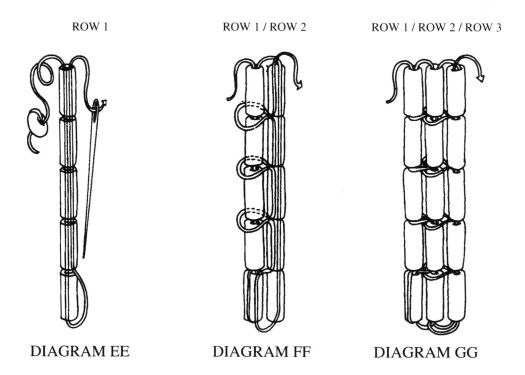

ROW 1   ROW 1 / ROW 2   ROW 1 / ROW 2 / ROW 3

DIAGRAM EE   DIAGRAM FF   DIAGRAM GG

Shaping Flat Weaves

You can add interest to the shape of woven beadwork by increasing or decreasing beads along the bottom edge of the weave. The following diagrams show the looping pattern for one- and two-bead increases and decreases.

Increasing or decreasing at the top edge of a woven piece is quite difficult and should be avoided because the resulting weave is messy-looking in comparison with the rest of the piece. If you work a piece that requires an uneven top edge, you should weave the bottom half of the piece first, then invert the partially completed weave and weave the remainder in reverse.

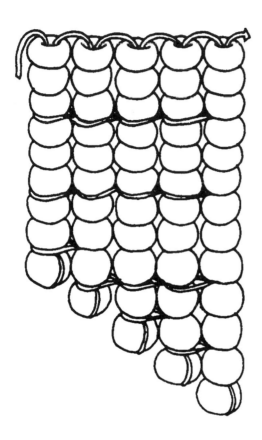

DIAGRAM HH

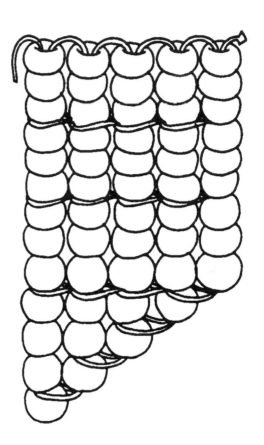

DIAGRAM II

This shows the basic pattern of loops when adding one bead to the length of a looped row. Note that the three-bead loop pattern is resumed in each row as soon as possible. Hangers may be added on increased rows.

This shows the basic pattern of loops for decreasing one bead at the bottom of a row. Be careful not to pull the thread too tightly, especially near the bottom bead.

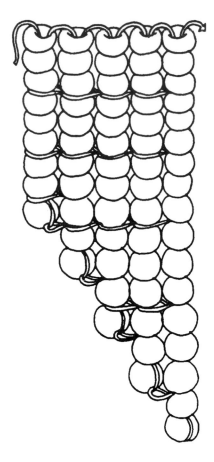

DIAGRAM JJ

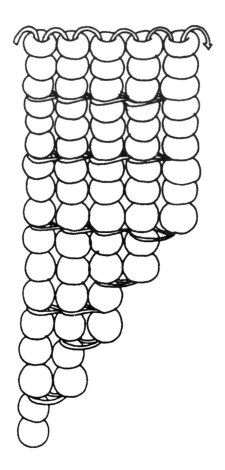

DIAGRAM KK

This shows the basic pattern of loops when adding two beads to the length of a looped row. Again, note that the three-bead looping pattern is resumed as soon as possible.

This shows the basic pattern of loops when decreasing two beads at the bottom of each row. Again, be careful to keep the thread tension taut but light.

Joining

When weaving a particularly large piece of beadwork, such as might be used in a purse or makeup case, it is easier to work small pieces and join them together; see Diagram LL. It is a good idea to use a very small needle for this procedure because the buildup of thread inside the bead holes can make it difficult to get a larger needle through. If you simply can not get the needle through, skip the clogged bead and go on to the next row. It will not be noticeable in the finished piece.

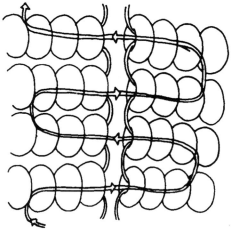

DIAGRAM LL

Fringes

When designs with fringes are patterned, there is a separation between the sections that show the foundation pattern and the fringe pattern.

When forming fringes, the tension of the thread is important. Try to leave enough slack so that the fringes move freely, but not so much that there is a lot of visible thread. Part of the beauty of fringes is their motion. If that motion is impeded by excessive thread tension, there will be something missing from the overall design.

The three-bead end (also know as a "picot") is worked by skipping the last three beads and running the needle back through the remaining beads on the fringe. Don't pull it too tightly, and try to settle the beads evenly at the end; see Diagram NN. Try using one color for the last four beads. It will form a diamond and give an interesting dimension to the design.

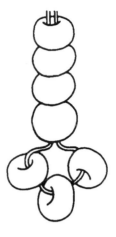

DIAGRAM NN

The simple one-bead end finish is worked by skipping the last bead and running the needle back through the remaining beads on the fringe. Be sure to nestle the bead sideways for a neat appearance; see Diagram OO.

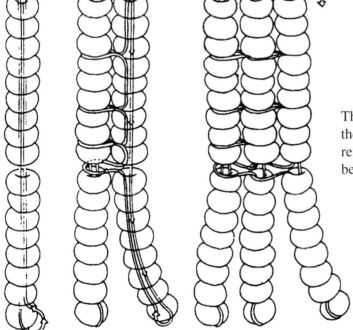

DIAGRAM MM

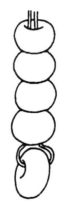

DIAGRAM OO

Finishing a Tube

Finishing a tube is simply a matter of securing the woven beadwork neatly around the foundation material of your choice. Ordinary clothesline is a nice foundation for a three-dimensional tube.

After all the weaving is completed, trim any excess threads that occur in the body of the weave. If there is a long piece of thread left at the end of the weave, use this to begin sewing the long edges together. Otherwise, bury a new thread within the weave at one end.

Cut a length of clothesline that will be at least 1" longer than the planned length of the tube. Wrap the woven length around the clothesline at the threaded end and weave the edges together. Line up the beads on one edge of the strip to the beads in the same row on the other edge of the strip; see Diagram PP.

Continue weaving back and forth until the entire length has been joined together. Trim the ends of the clothesline very closely to the end of the weave. It may be necessary to use a very small needle.

Finish the ends with seed beads that coordinate or complement the design of the piece you are finishing. Have the thread emerge from one of the beads on the outermost row of the weave on either end. Work rounds of beads according to the following instructions and Diagram QQ.

Round 1. Work two beads into each group of three beads around the end. This reduces the number of beads on the round from 18 to 12.

Round 2. Work one bead into each group of two beads in the round of 12 beads. This reduces the number of beads from 12 to six.

Round 3. Run the thread through the remaining six beads and tighten it just so the gap closes. Do not pull it too tightly or the end will pucker. Bury the remaining thread in the weave (not the clothesline) and trim it.

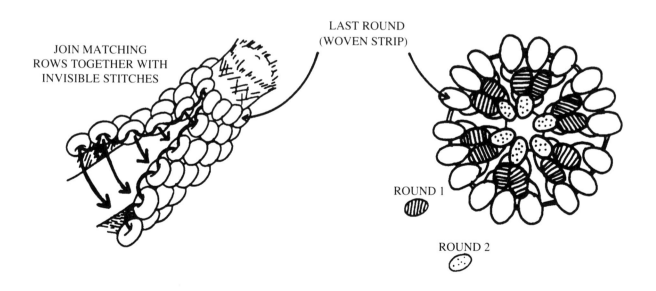

JOIN MATCHING ROWS TOGETHER WITH INVISIBLE STITCHES

LAST ROUND (WOVEN STRIP)

ROUND 1

ROUND 2

DIAGRAM PP

DIAGRAM QQ

Attaching Backing

To finish the back of woven projects, you will need scissors, lightweight cardboard (such as a piece of cereal box), common pins, needle and thread, fabric that coordinates with the beaded piece and tacky glue.

1. Lay the finished beadwork face down on the cardboard. Insert pins into the cardboard at the corners of the woven piece to mark the shape; see Diagram RR.

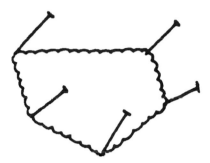

DIAGRAM RR

2. Connect the dots, then cut the cardboard about ⅛" smaller all around than the marked shape; see Diagram SS.

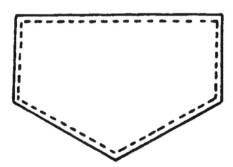

DIAGRAM SS

3. Using the cut cardboard as a guide, cut a piece of fabric with a margin of about ½" all around. Notch fabric at all corners; see Diagram TT.

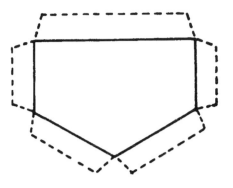

DIAGRAM TT

4. Center the cut cardboard shape on the fabric. Put several small dots of glue on the back of the fabric. Fold the edges of the fabric over the cardboard and glue the edges lightly; see Diagram UU.

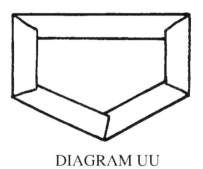

DIAGRAM UU

5. Position the fabric-covered cardboard on the back of the beadwork. Secure it to the beadwork with small invisible stitches; see Diagram VV. When attaching a pinback or barrette, sew right through the cardboard, if possible.

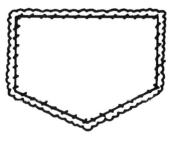

DIAGRAM VV

Bead Types

OPAQUE—solid color throughout the entire bead, usually somewhat matte in appearance, or with a dull gloss. Effective when used in Native American design.

LUSTERED—either opaque or transparent, these beads have a shiny finish (sometimes gold) applied to the outside surface of the bead. Good selection of colors available; run small.

CEYLON—opaque beads with a milky luminescent surface. Can appear similar to lustered beads, but slightly cloudier. Run small, with a high percentage of misshapen or irregular beads. Buy extras.

IRIS—opaque beads with a slightly metallic look. Iridescent finish on the surface. Widely used because of their rich look and design versatility. Most widely used colors are green, blue, and purple mixed iris. Copper, bronze, and red iris are gorgeous beads, but quite costly.

RAINBOW—similar to iris but transparent. Lighter colors than metallic look iris; can appear crystalline, almost opalescent depending on the predominant glass color.

TRANSPARENT—simple glass, clear with no finish added. Tend to be irregular in size, with smaller holes. Darker colors (especially blue and green) can appear cloudy.

SILVER-LINED—transparent beads of any color with the hole lined in silver. Usually available in square-holed or round-holed. Square-holed are easier to weave because the holes tend to be larger.

METALLIC—beads coated with any metallic color finish. The coatings are fragile and will rub off if handled roughly. Can be badly affected by finger oils. However, if carefully handled, they are effective and beautiful.

COLOR-LINED—transparent beads of any color with the hole lined in another color. The color of the outer glass will dominate. Holes can be small.

#2 BUGLES—can be woven with 11 seed beads. Substitute one #2 bugle for three seed beads. Widely available in silver-lined, iris, and rainbow.

#3 BUGLES—are best woven by themselves because they do not fit easily with seed beads within a woven pattern. Try them as part of a fringe or hanger.

11/0 SEED BEADS—are ideal for needleweaving. Can be mixed with #2 bugles.

10/0 SEED BEADS—are excellent for needleweaving. Check uniformity of size.

8/0 SEED BEADS—are good for use in graphic-type designs where strength is a factor.

6/0 SEED BEADS—can be woven, but are heavy to wear. Try using them as embellishments on hangers or fringes.

*M*etric Equivalency Chart

MM-Millimetres   CM-Centimetres

INCHES TO MILLIMETRES AND CENTIMETRES

INCHES	MM	CM	INCHES	CM	INCHES	CM
⅛	3	0.3	9	22.9	30	76.2
¼	6	0.6	10	25.4	31	78.7
½	13	1.3	12	30.5	33	83.8
⅝	16	1.6	13	33.0	34	86.4
¾	19	1.9	14	35.6	35	88.9
⅞	22	2.2	15	38.1	36	91.4
1	25	2.5	16	40.6	37	94.0
1¼	32	3.2	17	43.2	38	96.5
1½	38	3.8	18	45.7	39	99.1
1¾	44	4.4	19	48.3	40	101.6
2	51	5.1	20	50.8	41	104.1
2½	64	6.4	21	53.3	42	106.7
3	76	7.6	22	55.9	43	109.2
3½	89	8.9	23	58.4	44	111.8
4	102	10.2	24	61.0	45	114.3
4½	114	11.4	25	63.5	46	116.8
5	127	12.7	26	66.0	47	119.4
6	152	15.2	27	68.6	48	121.9
7	178	17.8	28	71.1	49	124.5
8	203	20.3	29	73.7	50	127.0

YARDS TO METRES

YARDS	METRES	YARDS	METRES	YARDS	METRES	YARDS	METRES	YARDS	METRES
⅛	0.11	2⅛	1.94	4⅛	3.77	6⅛	5.60	8⅛	7.43
¼	0.23	2¼	2.06	4¼	3.89	6¼	5.72	8¼	7.54
⅜	0.34	2⅜	2.17	4⅜	4.00	6⅜	5.83	8⅜	7.66
½	0.46	2½	2.29	4½	4.11	6½	5.94	8½	7.77
⅝	0.57	2⅝	2.40	4⅝	4.23	6⅝	6.06	8⅝	7.89
¾	0.69	2¾	2.51	4¾	4.34	6¾	6.17	8¾	8.00
⅞	0.80	2⅞	2.63	4⅞	4.46	6⅞	6.29	8⅞	8.12
1	0.91	3	2.74	5	4.57	7	6.40	9	8.23
1⅛	1.03	3⅛	2.86	5⅛	4.69	7⅛	6.52	9⅛	8.34
1¼	1.14	3¼	2.97	5¼	4.80	7¼	6.63	9¼	8.46
1⅜	1.26	3⅜	3.09	5⅜	4.91	7⅜	6.74	9⅜	8.57
1½	1.37	3½	3.20	5½	5.03	7½	6.86	9½	8.69
1⅝	1.49	3⅝	3.31	5⅝	5.14	7⅝	6.97	9⅝	8.80
1¾	1.60	3¾	3.43	5¾	5.26	7¾	7.09	9¾	8.92
1⅞	1.71	3⅞	3.54	5⅞	5.37	7⅞	7.20	9⅞	9.03
2	1.83	4	3.66	6	5.49	8	7.32	10	9.14

Index